MW00681501

Faith in the Public Square

Robert D. Cornwall

Living Faithfully in 21st Century America

Energion Publications

Gonzalez, Florida

2012

ISBN10: 1-893729-46-X
ISBN13: 978-1-893729-46-9
Library of Congress Control Number: 2012934827

Energion Publications
P. O. Box 841
Gonzalez, FL 32560

850-525-3916
www.energionpubs.com

This book is dedicated to the people of
First Christian Church (Disciples of Christ)
of Lompoc, CA and
Central Woodward Christian
(Disciples of Christ) of Troy, MI,
who have joined me in living faithfully in the
public square.

TABLE OF CONTENTS

FOREWORD

Richard Rorty, a leading philosophical pragmatist, has argued that there must be a strict separation between religion and public life to protect the values of a liberal democratic society. It may be okay for "idiosyncratic loves," like religious faith, to prevail in private life. But, for the good of the public, religion needs to remain privatized. Whenever religion enters the public sphere, claims Rorty, "it is a conversation-stopper."[1] Of course, especially given the activities of some leaders within the religious right in the United States since the 1970s, we have all seen instances where religion has publicly seemed to stop the conversation. This happens whenever a person of religious conviction enters a public debate with some kind of faith claim, but, when pressed for clear rationale or a reasoned elaboration, simply relies on "Because the Bible says so" as the entirety of an explanation. Of course, political leaders have also occasionally claimed a hard line in public, completely assured that their answers are right, without being able or willing to provide more reasonable support. Certain kinds of politics can stop a public conversation as quickly as certain types of religion can.

The main problem with Rorty's description of religion as a conversation-stopper is that it demonstrates that Rorty has a rather narrow-minded and distorted view of religion. He believes that religion can only speak in one way, the way that stops a conversation. But religion is far more complex and multifaceted

---

1   Rorty, "Religion as Conversation-Stopper," *Philosophy and Social Hope* (London: Penguin Books, 1999), p. 170-171. Originally, the essay appeared in *Common Knowledge* (Spring 1994): 1-6.

than such a view would indicate. The damage religion can cause in public is when it enters in such a way as to claim sole ownership to the truth, and then seeks to legislate its view of the truth so that it affects the rights of others, whether at home or abroad. This problem in approach, however, is not confined solely to religious people; anyone in possession of any kind of background, religious or not, can claim to know the truth in absolute ways, refusing to provide clear reasoning that others could understand or share.

Rorty is right about something else though. His life's work emphasizes the importance of history. No one, whether a person of religious faith or not, can "escape from the finitude of one's time and place."[2] Truth is always a human enterprise. And it is forever created by, and contained within, the confines of human language. This means we must always be aware that when we describe what we believe to be truth, we are using the confines of human language to do so. Truth transcends our ability to describe it with precision and complete accuracy. As is true when Christians attempt to describe God, all we can do in describing truth is point, we hope with some degree of accuracy, in the general direction of it. In a sense, whether we are truly religious or not, we are living out our "faith" in the fact that we are describing what is true when we speak about truth. We can certainly create very strong and reasonable justifications for why we believe something to be true. Yet, in the end, we must allow for the possibility that some distance might remain between our justifications about what we believe to be true and truth itself.[3] When religious individuals and groups are able to understand the difference between justification and truth, they are ready to enter the public debate with integrity and in a way that proves their voices can provide added value for dealing with the complex issues facing public life.

---

2   For the quote, see Rorty, *Consequences of Pragmatism* (Minneapolis: University of Minnesota Press, 1982), p. xix.

3   Jeffrey Stout makes this case in *Ethics After Babel: The Languages of Morals and Their Discontents* (Boston: Beacon Press, 1988), 22-32, and 82-103.

Bob Cornwall's musings presented here are ample evidence that considerable benefit can be derived when religion assumes a public voice. In fact, Cornwall's hope for these essays, as noted in the "Introduction," is that they will "start a conversation, not end it." And the book certainly accomplishes that task. Readers will find it easy to converse with these essays. As Cornwall maps a journey across topics contained in the religious landscape, the vast varieties of faith, the ideologies associated with both politics and faith, and American hopes for justice in the land, he provides a sensitive religious voice, one tempered by humility and characterized by a tone of respect for difference. The good people of Lompoc, California found this public religious voice refreshing. I've got every confidence that the readers of this book will appreciate it as well. In fact, my hope is that these essays might motivate a plethora of religious voices to join the chorus. The many voices of religion, and here I mean all religious voices – not just those associated with Christianity, must become responsibly public, relevant, and, above all, reasonable if all of us in North America are going to be able to navigate successfully the territory being created by the most significant issues facing us in our day.

Mark G. Toulouse
Principal, Emmanuel College of Victoria University
in the University of Toronto

PREFACE

For nearly four years I wrote a weekly column that appeared on the Sunday Op-Ed page of the *Lompoc Record*. Knowing that the column needed some kind of identifying title I chose to call it *Faith in the Public Square*. What I desired to show in this column was that, despite the claims of some that the public square was naked (that is without the presence of the voices of those who profess faith), faith is present in the public square and that it can have a constructive role in a square that has become increasingly pluralistic. As I took up this position of Sunday commentator, I kept in mind the fact that I wasn't writing for the church page, which appeared on Fridays. My job was not to sermonize or deal with churchy topics, but instead I would need to address issues that faced the broader public. And so, I took up issues like politics, government, science, and education. Yes, I took up religious issues as well, but I tried to do so in a way that took into account the breadth of religious options present in the community, even as I spoke from within my own faith tradition. That is, I didn't just write for Christians, but for all people of faith.

What I discovered from my efforts at being a public commentator is that there were many people in the community, many of whom had long before written off religious faith, who found this column helpful and attractive. I was even called upon to do a funeral for a regular reader whom I had never met, but who found sustenance in the column. There is a place for faith in the public square but if this voice is to be heard it has to be offered in a way that is respectful to the views of those who differ in view, especially those who may not affirm a faith position. The point is not to defend the faith, but rather to speak to important issues from the perspective of faith.

For some time I've wanted to gather some of these columns together and publish them in a more organized fashion. The majority of these brief essays that you have before you were originally written as op-ed articles for the Lompoc Record. Some of them dealt with issues of the moment, others were written to address those issues that continually face us as we live as people of faith in the public square. I have tried to choose pieces to share here that even when dealing with issues of the moment have a more universal application. For the most part, these columns are presented here as they originally appeared in the paper. The majority of adjustments, beyond simple editing, were made in order to make them more time and context sensitive.

I realize that when one reads a book like this that not every essay will touch a reader in the same way, and therefore some readers may find it more effective to browse through the book, stopping at those spots that are speaking to them at the moment. However you decide to read the book my hope is that these essays will prove challenging and transformative.

As I invite you, the reader, to begin the journey through this book, there are a number of people that require a word of appreciation. I want to begin with my original editor at the *Lompoc Record*, Bo Poertner. He took a chance by giving over the primary editorial spot on Sunday mornings to a pastor. I appreciated his words of encouragement and guidance over the course of the years that I wrote for the paper – as well as the conversations over breakfast that occurred during this period of time. I need to also thank the people of First Christian Church (Disciples of Christ) of Lompoc, California, who not only gave me the freedom to write this column, but did so joyously. Amy Haithcoat made sure that a copy of the column made it up on the bulletin board each Sunday before the church service even began. Then there's the Rev. Bill Denton, the retired pastor of that congregation, who served with me as minister of visitation. Early on Bill offered his services as proof reader. I'm glad I took him up on the offer, as his comments not only improved the grammar, but the content as well. I didn't always follow his advice, but I always took his suggestions into consideration. I should also give a word of thanks to Joyce

Howerton, the former mayor of Lompoc and a good friend, who encouraged me to pursue this venture with the Record. Now that we've reached the point of publishing in book form this collection, I would like to thank Henry Neufeld for not only publishing this book, but for being willing to publish a series of books that I've written. And, as they say, any written work requires the attention of more than one person! Words of gratitude must be extended to my current congregation, Central Woodward Christian Church (Disciples of Christ) of Troy, Michigan, which has allowed me the freedom to live my faith in public. Finally, I would like to again give thanks to my wife Cheryl who has lovingly helped me keep a broader life focus for more than twenty-eight years, even as I've tried to give voice to these values and concerns.

INTRODUCTION:
LIVING A PUBLIC FAITH
IN THE PUBLIC SQUARE

Nearly three decades ago Richard John Neuhaus wrote a book with an arresting title – *The Naked Public Square*. Neuhaus' argument was simple – religion is in danger of losing its traditional place in the public square, or rather the public square was in danger of losing the leavening agency of religion. In his estimation, the United States was following the lead of Europe in becoming a secularized nation. One could argue that Neuhaus misdiagnosed the problem, since religion – at least in its more conservative forms – remains a constant presence in public life. Although religious voices continue to make themselves heard, there is clear evidence that religion, especially in its institutionalized forms, is in a decades-long retreat. Therefore, Neuhaus may have been on to something, but the reasons for the shrinking back of the religious voice may have less to do with organized efforts to marginalise religion and more the fact that religion has lost relevance to the public square.

The decline in the influence and presence of institutional religion has been shown in numerous surveys and polls, but a visit to the nation's houses of worship is sufficient proof. It appears that a majority of our houses of worship are populated by persons over fifty, if not older. That there are mega-churches across the country filled to capacity should not lead the reader to believe that this represents the majority of Americans. Yes, the vast majority of Americans believe in God, but a small minority of them visits houses of worship. Indeed, the fastest growing religious group in America has been called the "nones." That is, they do not belong to any formal religious community. That is not to say that this "group," which tends to be younger in age, isn't interested in spiritual things; it just means that they don't have much use for institutional forms of religion (Neuhaus).[1] One reason that is often given for why so many young adults find institutional religion distasteful is that they believe that it is too politicized.[2]

Although I don't believe that the public square has been completely emptied of religious content, I do believe we've moved beyond the point where any one particular faith tradition can dominate public life, as Protestantism did for much of the nation's history. There are simply too many different voices clamoring to be heard, not all of which are distinctly religious.

When we talk about religion in public life, we tend to think in political terms. It is true that when religion is present in public that presence often has political implications, but that doesn't mean that every form of religious presence must be political. I appreciate the distinction that Parker Palmer makes between private, public, and political spheres. Leaving aside the issue of the private sphere, it is important to remember that the public sphere is larger than the political, which is focused on the exercise of power. The public arena is that place where the stranger is present and welcome. It is that sphere where we meet others for education, conversation, work, politics, the sharing of culture and religious life. It is the place where civic life occurs, and it is in this place that we discern that we're in this together. Parker's concern is that there is an increasing trend for us to retreat to the private sphere where strangers are welcome only upon invitation. Such a movement away living in the public square has political implications and can be detrimental to democratic practices (Palmer, 89-117).

When I speak here of faith in the public square I do have politics in mind, but I'm more focused on the broader public

---

1   On the current religious situation in America see Robert D. Putnam and David E. Campbell, *American Grace: How Religion Divides and Unites Us*, (New York: Simon and Schuster, 2010), pp. 120-132.

2   For an interesting discussion of faith and politics from the perspective of progressively minded young adults see Amy Gopp, Christian Piatt, and Brandon Gilvin, eds., *Split Ticket: Independent Faith in a Time of Partisan Politics*. (St. Louis: Chalice Press, 2010).

sphere, where strangers, as well as friends and family gather, as a community, in all of our differences and similarities. Perhaps the best way to understand this public realm is to consider Palmer's definition of citizenship:

> Citizenship is a way of being in the world rooted in the knowledge that I am a member of a vast community of human and nonhuman beings that I depend on for essentials I could never provide for myself (*Ibid*, 31).

As a member of this community that is local and global, the question is – am I committed to the goal of working toward the common good? This question has political implications, but it's not only a matter of politics. It is also a question that raises issues of faith, which is most assuredly personal, but not necessarily private. What I believe and why I believe is a matter of great personal concern, but if my faith is meaningful then surely it must have something to say to the way I live in the public realm. So the real question that faces us today concerns the manner in which we bring our faith into the public square.[3]

As people of faith ponder the possibility of engaging the public sphere as people of faith, they must recognize the inherent dangers of that engagement. History is full of examples of unfortunate entanglements. More often than not faith is jettisoned as people and institutions become enamored with power. Politics, by its very nature, is the "art of the possible," which means that it inevitably requires compromise, especially in a democracy. History is also replete with examples of nations co-opting religion, especially during time of war. Even relatively liberal churches find it difficult to break free of nationalistic interests. There is no better symbol of this reality than the very fact that most churches have an

---

3   On the ways in which Christianity relates to public life see Mark Toulouse, *God in Public: Four Ways American Christianity and Public Life Relate.* (Louisville: WJK Press, 2006). Building on this book is an article I wrote with Arthur Gross Schaefer, "Faith and Politics: Finding a Way to Have a Fruitful Conversation" *Congregations* (Summer 2008): 27-30.

American flag in their sanctuary – often sitting near the front, for all to see. It's seen as well in the fact that for many, nationalistic songs are as popular on Independence Day as Christmas carols are during the Christmas season! It is, therefore, understandable that there would be calls for the church to step back from an engagement with the public arena, perhaps even declaring partisan politics to be anathema to one's faith.

The Anabaptist tradition, for which I have great respect, offers us an excellent example of a tradition that has sought to separate itself from much of the traditional political realm, while remaining committed to the common good. The witness of people like John Howard Yoder and Stanley Hauerwas, who have suggested alternate ways of engaging the world that seek to remain separate from these traditional political forces, has made itself felt even outside traditional Anabaptist circles. Their warnings about getting cozy with the political realm are worth listening to, even if one, me included, has not abandoned the possibility of engaging with the political system in pursuit of the common good (Bevere).

I understand why some of my co-religionists have chosen to stay clear of government entanglements, though I'm not convinced that it's possible to work for justice or work for the common good without engaging the political system in some way. It is for this reason that I have involved myself in efforts to engage elected officials in conversation and when necessary even pressuring them to do what I believe would be the right thing. Additionally, even as I recognize that political parties are not perfect instruments, I have chosen to support one of the two major parties and its candidates for office during elections. It's not that I believe God favors one party over the other, but I do believe that one party better fits my own understanding of the common good, an understanding that is informed by my faith.

Even as I align myself with one of America's two political parties and accept the realities of being a citizen of a particular nation, I'm also cognizant that I'm called to give allegiance not to the flag or the nation for which it stands, but to God who transcends national interests. That is, if I faithfully pray the Lord's Prayer then I must give full and complete allegiance to God and to God's realm. Whatever I do in the public sphere must be done in the light of that prior commitment.[4] Remaining faithful to one's ultimate allegiance, while engaging the public square, is not an easy task. It requires humility and a willingness to recognize that not everyone shares my beliefs or values. My goal in engaging the public square isn't purely religious; that is, while my goal is not to impose my faith on the populace as a whole, I am committed to being present in the public square, which involves political action. This political action is informed by my faith. I may engage it as a private citizen, which allows more partisan engagement, or I may come to the square as part of the faith community, but in this case the engagement should be less partisan or even non-partisan.

One of the reasons why it is difficult for people to enter the public square and remain faithful their religious beliefs, is that we're often required to compromise to get things done. Often we cast aside our principles in the name of gaining a greater good. We may believe that something is wrong or not in line with God's desire – perhaps going to war – but we're willing to go along because we have other priorities that we believe need to be achieved. Or, maybe we just don't want to make waves. Another reason why many people find it difficult to either engage the public square from a faith perspective or make room for a faith perspective is that much of the current conversation is couched in terms of a culture war or more globally as a clash of civilizations. This makes conversation difficult, and it makes it even more difficult for people to work together for the common good, since there's always suspicion that the other might be an "enemy combatant."

Often we find that people living on both sides of the political chasm believe that there are sinister forces afoot who are seeking

4   On the question of allegiance see my book *Ultimate Allegiance: The Subversive Nature of the Lord's Prayer*, (Gonzalez, FL: Energion Publications, 2010).

to impose their agenda on society. In some ways, they're right; there are groups seeking to impose their agenda on society, but in a democracy we have, or should have the freedom, to resist an ideology/agenda that we find in appropriate. The problem we face today isn't differences of opinion as to the right direction for the nation, but the way in which we have demonized each other (Palmer, 16). Some of this polarization has religious elements to it, making it increasingly difficult for people to work together to find solutions to our problems as a nation and as a world.

Because we live in an era of dramatic changes, and to be honest, increasing secularism, we have seen reactionary efforts that hearken back to what is believed by some to be a golden age when traditional values held sway over America. This golden age was the 1950s, when a White Anglo-Saxon Protestant cultural hegemony continued to hold sway. That hegemony began to crumble in the 1960s, and the golden age has been shown to be more myth than reality. Whatever the realities of the 1950s, our realities are much different and the value of returning to that age, even if it was "simpler," isn't something that many of us would welcome. The nation today is much more diverse than before, especially in its public life, as both women and ethnic minorities have found their way into the public square. As for religion, it may no longer be the "in-thing," but there is not only more religious pluralism, but religion has ceased to be something we join up with simply for its social benefits. If we choose to join a faith community, it will because that faith community speaks to our spiritual realities.

People of faith, if they choose to enter the public square, face the question of why they are making this move into public life. There are those who desire either to dominate public life through the imposition of religious law or a theological vision, whether that is Sharia, the Ten Commandments, or the Sermon on the Mount! Others hope to gain special privileges, whether that involves official establishment or some other form of support. American history shows that there was not a consensus on this question, even as the states began to ratify the Constitution.

In the essays that comprise this book I hope to create a conversation that would help the nation in which I live, as well as the global society, to work together for the common good. I happen to believe that while it has its flaws, the American political system is the best system yet devised. It is a democratic system, and yet it has imposed checks and balances that have provided political stability. This is the context in which citizens, including people of faith engage each other publicly. The US Constitution allows for people of faith to exercise their faith in public. There are few legal prohibitions of religious practice in America, and the government must show a compelling reason for limiting religious speech and activity (usually matters relating to personal or public safety). Therefore, the government, according to the First Amendment, cannot either impose a religious orthodoxy on the nation or infringe on the rights of religious people to practice their faith openly. These are very important rights that bring with them important responsibilities. Therefore, people of faith must enter the public square boldly but respectfully, for there is more than one viewpoint on matters religious and non-religious present in the public square. That said, from the perspective of faith, one must ask the question – what kind of world does my faith tradition envision and how should a person of faith seek to bring this vision to fruition?

As we seek to understand how this question of vision is worked out in public, we must remember that this is a pluralistic democracy and that the players in the public square must respect the rights of the other. There are rules that govern our engagement with the public square. Sometimes we may decide that the issues closest to our hearts require us to trespass the boundaries, and be willing to suffer the consequences. The notion of nonviolent civil disobedience is a recognized form of expression in our society, and without it the Civil Rights Movement would never have achieved the results it sought.

I would argue that religion has an important role to play in public life, because in its institutional forms at least, religion is a public entity. It is a public space where people come together, linked by a common faith, but generally emerging from outside a particular family grouping. It is a public space where people can join and leave if they choose. Some religious communities are more engaged with the public sphere than others, but all have a place in public life. As a public entity, my belief is that each faith community has an opportunity to contribute to the common good of the nation and the world. That is, if we believe that faith transcends family and nation, then it calls us to embrace the good of the entire creation.

Our conversation about the proper role of faith in the public square must take into consideration the existence of America's civil religion – a religion that has historically reflected a Protestant Christian ethos even though Christianity has never been officially acknowledged as the nation's established faith. Of course, it's not as if no one has tried to establish America as a Christian nation, only that they've never succeeded in legally enacting such a law. America's civil religion often uses icons of this dominant faith tradition, mixing them in with more political or nationalist icons, to give support to nationalist hopes and dreams. Another way in which this civil religion has been expressed is through the use of providentialist language, which is most clearly expressed in the ideas of Manifest Destiny and American Exceptionalism.

America's civil religion is perhaps best expressed in the current national motto "In God We Trust." This motto replaced the more expansive "*e pluribus unum*" in 1956, at the same time as the phrase "one nation under God" was added to the Pledge of Allegiance. Other examples of civil religion include the presence of chaplains in Congress (to this point always Christian, and generally Protestant), the ubiquitous use of the phrase "God Bless America" by American politicians, and the singing of "God Bless America" during the seventh inning stretch after 9-11.

All of this suggests that a significant number of Americans want to claim divine blessings for the nation's hopes and dreams. Of course, some would go further and establish this "civil religion" in a specifically Christian form. At the same time there are religious voices that rail against the use of religion to prop up nationalist dreams. Some call for the faith community to remove itself from the public square entirely, abandoning public life to other voices and groups, while others wish to remain separate enough from the national ethos that they can "speak truth to power." And some would offer an alternative voice that warns Americans about the danger to authentic faith when church and state become too cozy, or warning that a coercive religion can have unfortunate impact on America's liberty.

It is interesting that at the dawn of the nation's history rationalists and evangelicals made common cause in support of religious liberty. Perhaps the best example of this realization can be seen in Thomas Jefferson's letter to the Danbury Association of Baptists, where the famed religious skeptic and author of the Declaration of Independence spoke of the now famous wall of separation:

> Believing with you that religion is a matter which lies solely between man and his God, that he owes account to none other for his faith or his worship, that the legislative powers of government reach actions only, and not opinions, I contemplate with sovereign reverence that act of the whole American people which declared that their legislature should 'make no law respecting an establishment of religion, or prohibiting the free exercise thereof,' thus building a wall of separation between church and State.[5]

While Jefferson and Madison sought to build safeguards into the national conversation that would protect minority voices, there were other voices that sought to keep religion and government tightly linked. Those arguing for this linkage tended to fear what would happen to the "moral" foundations of the nation if church

---

5   Thomas Jefferson, "Letter to the Danbury Baptist Association," 1802, (http://www.loc.gov/loc/lcib/9806/danpre.html)

and state were severed. Of course, to this point in history there
were few examples of the kind of religious freedom that Jefferson
and Baptist leader John Leland were advocating.

As we look back to the founding of the American nation we
need to disabuse ourselves of two myths. One myth holds that the
founders were all Christians who sought to create a Christian
nation. This is a myth propagated by many conservative Christians.
The second myth suggests that the majority of the founders were
secularists, or at most Deists. The reality is much more complex.
Franklin and possibly Jefferson were Deists, though Jefferson's
belief that the hand of providence was at work in the forming of
the nation raises questions about that appellation. John Adams
wasn't orthodox by evangelical standards, but as a devout Unitarian
(a form of Christian liberalism) he believed that religion did have
a role in society. It's also worth noting that the 1800 election
between Jefferson and Adams offered interesting religious
overtones that were as divisive then as they are today. Adam's
cousin, Samuel, on the other hand would be considered an
evangelical today, as would John Jay and Patrick Henry. So, as we
ponder this question of religion's role in society it's best to
recognize the historical complexity of this issue.

A close reading of American history will lead to the recognition
that religious and secular forces have often jostled with each other
for dominance. And there is considerable evidence that Protestant
forces worked hard at keeping themselves the dominant force in
American life. Yes, there was to be diversity in practice and even
theology, but even religious liberals feared the prospect of their
loss of dominance. Over the course of time, most Americans have
accepted the idea that this nation has inherited a political order that
has been influenced by both religious and secular ideals. As western
Europeans it is natural that the Founders would be influenced by
Jewish and Christian traditions – including the Ten
Commandments. But they were also influenced by Enlightenment
principles, which often drew upon classical Greek and Roman
ideals. While some early American leaders sought official

recognition of the United States as a Christian nation, that view didn't prevail in the end. At the same time there was a consensus among the early Founders that religion had a role to play in public life, although that influence was less theological than it was moral and ethical. Figures such as Washington and Adams were most concerned about the promotion of virtue, and they believed that religion could provide the foundation for this necessary component of a self-governing democracy.

————————————

With this collection of essays I seek to affirm the value that religious faith brings to the public square. If, as appears to be true, the secular city is giving way to a post-secular city, where spirituality and religiosity is increasingly present, even if not always in institutional forms, it is important to have a conversation about what this looks like and how it will be present in our society. At at its best, religion provides a moral vision for society, but it can easily fall into a self-righteous moralism. In its congregational forms, religion can provide a context in which people learn how to live in community. However, if people of faith are to find a place in the public square they will have to know the rules. These rules, especially in the diverse and pluralist American context, call on us to honor the diversity and pluralism. It means respecting the voice of the other, even when we disagree on matters of religion.

We are to respect the other, but there are limits. Not every view or perspective deserves to be welcomed into the public square. While we can vigorously debate issues of great importance, there is no place for demonizing the other. Voices of bigotry and hatred need to be confronted and opposed. This is especially true when such voices lead to the marginalization of people or to violence. When religion is used to support such perspectives, then we need to call into question the inherent value of those religious views. In my mind, at its best, religion will contribute to the common good. It will enter the public realm with humility.

My concern, as expressed in the op-ed columns I wrote for *Lompoc Record*, was to give voice to the perspectives held by moderate and liberal religious adherents. Unfortunately, these voices tend to get drowned out by the often bitter debates between extremists at either end of the spectrum. I also sought to advocate for the inclusion of other faith traditions in the public conversation. In op-ed columns and in my blog posts, I have tried to provide an alternative vision of how faith and public life might interact with each other, arguing that the public square is impoverished both when the religious voice is absent, and when only one voice is present.

I also wrote from the perspective that if faith is to have any real value then it must influence the public life of its adherents. I understand why John F. Kennedy felt he had to draw a line between his religious views and his role as President, but surely the principles of his faith had some influence on his political beliefs and actions, especially when it comes to providing an ethical and moral grounding to his decisions, even if these understandings had to be expressed in more secular clothing. I'm also not so naïve to believe that many people serving in public life don't act in ways that run quite contrary to the teachings of their faith. Indeed, we have a tendency to pick and choose those beliefs that support our positions and ignore the other.

Because we live in a religiously pluralistic context, the vision that is expressed by people of faith for their community needs to be expressed in ways that can be affirmed by people across the breadth of religious and non-religious citizens. Our values should be rooted in our faith traditions but they also must be translated into non-religious specific language. This is the point that President Barack Obama made in 2008 speech to the Call to Renewal Meeting, while still a candidate for the presidency.

> Democracy demands that the religiously motivated translate their concerns into universal, rather than religion-specific, values. It requires that their proposals be subject to argument, and amenable to reason. I may be opposed to abortion for religious reasons, but if I seek to pass a law banning the

practice, I cannot simply point to the teachings of my church or evoke God's will. I have to explain why abortion violates some principle that is accessible to people of all faiths, including those with no faith at all.[6]

Does this mean that we do not speak clearly and unequivocally from our faith? No, but, if we wish to enact laws that affect the lives of all citizens, no matter their religious perspective, then we must do more than simply say "the Bible says." There will, of course, be times when we must speak to the Public Square from an explicitly theological/faith-based perspective, but in doing so recognize that the hearer may not give authority to the source of one's perspective. But, more often than not, when we come into the square and use explicitly theological/religious language we are speaking not to those outside our faith, but to those who share our faith. Even there, we must be careful to speak with humility and respect, two qualities that are not always present in our midst.

Those who, like me, are Christians need to be especially circumspect about their behavior when entering the public square. Being the majority faith, even if this faith tradition is as diverse and varied as the Christian faith, gives considerable power to those who seek to speak in this square. The power of numbers cannot be easily discounted, which makes the claims that Christians in America are facing persecution rather implausible. Being asked to say "Happy Holidays" by one's employer doesn't represent an infringement on one's ability to celebrate one's faith, nor does the ban on school sponsored prayer limit the ability of Christians to express their faith. All that these limitations on our "freedom" do is provide a more equal and equitable space for people of all faiths – or no faith at all – to live safely and contentedly in this nation.

---

6 Barak Obama, *Call to Renewal* speech, June 28, 2008 (http://obamaspeeches.com/081-Call-to-Renewal-Keynote-Address-Obama-Speech.htm)

What follows is a discussion of religion, culture, politics, social issues, that assumes an interaction between faith and the public square. These conversations are loosely grouped together around the following areas of discussion: The Religious Landscape; Varieties of Faith – a Common Cause; Politics, Ideology, and Faith; Justice in the Land.

Many of them were time/context sensitive, and all were written with the broader public in mind, not just the religious communities – that is, they appeared on the Sunday Opinion page rather than on the Friday Church page. They were intended to start a conversation in the community, and this collection, whether read straight through or piece meal, is designed to start a conversation, not end it. The reader then is invited to consider what it means to live faithfully in public. For the most part, these essays are published in the same form as the originally appeared, with the only adjustments besides grammatical ones being focused on making them more time and location appropriate. That is, if the essays addressed specific issues at the time, I have either generalized them or reset the context.

In closing this introductory statement, I should note that I write from a particular perspective. I'm white, male, fairly well-educated, Protestant, ordained, and politically and theologically left of center. Some readers may perceive what some call a Niebuhrian realism in my reflections. They are likely correct, though I've not read as widely in Reinhold Niebuhr's works as I'd like. Still, Niebuhr was known for his realist perspective, one that recognized that humanity has the potential for both good and evil. As I look at this world I am a realist, with an optimistic strain – probably more so than was true of Niebuhr. Since I write from a particular point of view that has developed/evolved over time, I do not expect the reader to agree with me at every point, but I hope that whether you read the book from cover or cover or pick and choose among the various offerings, that you will see these postings as an invitation to a conversation about ways in which people of faith can work together to create a better world (even if we must recognize that such a reality likely won't happen in our life time or due to our own efforts). With that in mind I entrust this book and the readers to the grace of God.

THE RELIGIOUS LANDSCAPE

"The Times They Are a-Changin'"

"The times they are a-changin'," so sang Bob Dylan four decades back. Then as now change is the one constant in life. We may resist its charms, but there often comes a time when we long for something new and different. While the status quo will always have its defenders, ultimately history shows that such resistance to change will prove futile. Life is continually evolving.

While there seems to be a built in resistance to change, I believe that is because we fear the unknown. Even if the past is unpleasant, at least it's a known quantity. To embrace the call for change is a bit like "throwing dice." Can we afford to take the risk?

But progress requires that we take risks. Going into space was risky. So was leaving the confines of slavery in Egypt for the unknown prospects of the Promised Land. The question is: How do we go forward into the future without letting the voices of fear and pessimism pull us back into the clutches of the status quo? Should we choose to heed the voice of optimism and hope, perhaps history could be a helpful guide.

As every stock prospectus will tell you, history is no infallible indicator of the future. But if we take a broad look into the past we will notice two things. First, nothing stays the same for very long. Second, when difficult times have arisen people have *stepped* forward and found a *way* forward. Whether it is politics, economics, or matters of faith, there will be those who will continually remind us that the glass is half empty. Be careful, they'll say, that you don't get too far out in front of popular sentiment. But there are others who will see the future in broader, more hopeful terms. They can envision a world where violence, hatred, and anger don't dominate.

Although religion can reinforce the status quo — indeed institutional religion is often a partner to the status quo — faith can also empower us to look at the world with hopeful eyes. Such has been the case for me, as a follower of Jesus Christ.

This issue of change figures prominently in Walter Russell Mead's book *God and Gold: Britain, America, and the Making of the Modern World* (Knopf, 2007). He suggests that the future belongs to those willing to surf the wave of global change. Looking at the world historically, he finds that over the past three centuries, it has been the Anglo-American world that has proven itself best able to do just that. Whether this will continue to be true as we move into the future is an open question. There is significant evidence that places like China, whose systems and religious foundations are very different from those found in the West, seem more adept at surfing the current wave of change.

One of the issues addressed in the book is the role religion has played in forging the Anglo-American world view and how it has enabled people of faith to address the question of change. The son of a clergyman, Mead takes religion very seriously and recognizes that while religion can be a force for evil, it can also be a force for good in the world. The question is how.

Mead believes there are three competing visions operating in the world. The future is best served when these three are kept in balance. The key is what he calls the small "a" anglican model, a model he takes from Anglicanism, which has historically embraced a three-fold authority — Reason, Scripture, and Tradition. In this new model the three sources of authority name the three competing visions of reality: Reason (science/technology/rule of law), Religion, and Tradition (Nationalism/identity politics). When any one of these gets the upper hand, the results are often catastrophic, but if kept in balance they temper tendencies toward arrogance, exclusivism, division, and ultimately violence.

Looking at the world through the lens of my own faith, I see a future that is open but under the influence of God. I may not be totally comfortable with the image of Adam Smith's "Invisible Hand," but the idea of providence isn't a far-fetched idea. As we face the future, we have a choice. We can resist the fact that change is inevitable, or we can learn to surf the global wave of change in ways that bring benefit to the world in which we live. Religion can divide us, but if we will learn to live with our differences in belief and practice, we can join together and build a new community that is filled with justice, hope, and peace.

OUR CHANGING RELIGIOUS LANDSCAPE

The United States is among the most religiously observant nations in the world, with nearly 80% of us apparently professing some form of Christian faith. We are also one of the most religiously diverse nations in the world. While in theory this isn't a Christian nation, the dominant religion has been, since colonial times, Christian. That theoretical dominance continues to this day, but things are in flux, especially among the Protestant majority. The long standing dominance of Protestantism is being eroded by a number of forces, some of which lie outside its control. One of Protestantism's strengths and weaknesses is its diversity. When we think of Protestantism, there is no monolithic form that comes to mind. It can be liberal or conservative, politically active or apolitical. Some believe in evolution, others don't. Some are pacifist and others support the nation's military policies. It includes Episcopal and Pentecostal, Baptist and Methodist, and many more.

This diversity has allowed Protestantism to flourish in the midst of America's embrace of religious freedom. But things are changing. A half century ago, about the time I was born, two-thirds of Americans or more were Protestant, with what is known as Mainline Protestantism being the largest component of this majority. Roman Catholics, with about 25% of the population, made up the rest. When I was born, late in the 1950s, the country was at the tail end of a decade of "religious revival" that coincided with the end of a popularly supported war and the beginnings of a baby boom. At that time, nearly 60% of the population was actively affiliated with a Christian congregation. That was then, but today things have changed. The question is: Where are the trends leading?

Questions about the nation's changing religious identity were raised in a groundbreaking report published by the *Pew Forum on Religion and Public Life*. The study focuses on America's religious landscape, and its release was hailed on the pages of America's magazines and newspapers. Although all manner of people are interested in demographic studies like this – from advertisers to political advisers, religious leaders and clergy are the ones most interested in it. The report, which is based on interviews with 35,000 people, tells us some things many of us already knew or suspected. It reminds us that things are changing and that our allegiances are fluid. We may still be religious, but there's a growing number of those who, whether religious or not, are choosing to be unaffiliated.

The most telling statistics come from the nation's young adults – those aged 18-29. While 51% of Americans continue to be Protestant, only 43% of young adults make the same claim. The percentage of Catholics in America has remained relatively stable over the decades – standing at around 25% – but that stability is largely the result of increased immigration from Roman Catholic countries. Nearly a third of those raised Catholic are no longer Catholic – leaving about 10% of the population as former Catholics.

So, what's happening? The first thing to note is that many of us have been switching our religious allegiances. About 28% of us have changed the religious affiliation that we grew up with; if we count Protestants who have switched denominations, the number climbs to 44% (a number I think might be conservative). Although I've been a life-long Protestant, I'm part of that 44%. My own faith journey has taken me across the denominational and theological spectrum, so I understand the trend.

It's that growing number of "unaffiliated" (16%) that gets the attention of most religious leaders. It's not that our nation's young people are becoming atheists or agnostics. Despite the seeming popularity of vocal and often strident atheists such as Richard Dawkins, Christopher Hitchens, and Sam Harris, there are very few atheists in our midst (1.6%). Most are simply nothing in particular – some are spiritually inclined, while others aren't. Where these numbers are growing the fastest is among young adults under 30 (24%). That number is greater than the number of evangelicals, mainline Protestants, or Roman Catholics of the same age. It raises huge questions about the religious direction of the nation.

Now the nation isn't in danger of becoming a secular bastion like what we've seen develop in Europe. Just listen to the God-talk of our Presidential candidates – that should be enough to dispel the idea we're becoming an irreligious society. But things are very fluid and the trend is away from institutionalized religion – especially on the West Coast.

A NEW VOICE IN AMERICA–GENERATION NEXT

We've had the Baby Boomers, Generation X, and now we bid welcome to Generation Next (or the Millennial Generation – those under 30). Each generation has its own distinguishing marks and quirks, and marketers want to know everything they can about these generational shifts as they guide the development of everything from food products to cars. Political parties and religious groups also want to look at this data so they can better connect with target audiences. Understanding how people think and act can make a big difference in how we relate to the world in which we live and plan for the future.

So who makes up this next generation to emerge on the scene and come of age at this particular moment in history? Several years ago The Pew Research Center for the People and the Press released a report entitled *A Portrait of "Generation Next: How Young People View Their Lives, Futures and Politics* (January 2007). In this study, we learn that this technologically savvy generation is more liberal, more tolerant, and less religious than previous generations. This is also a marked generation, by which I mean, they have marked themselves physically – half of them are sporting tattoos, piercings, or untraditionally colored hair.

With the recent midterm elections (2006) fresh in our minds, it might be worth noting that whereas Gen X was the most Republican of recent generations, Generation Next may be the most Democratic (48% to 35%) in many a year. While not yet showing an inclination to vote in great numbers, they are very interested in politics, and should they vote in great numbers they could have significant impact on important issues facing the nation and the world. Though they don't vote in great numbers this generation seems less cynical about government and more trusting of government institutions.

Perhaps, therefore, it shouldn't be surprising that on social and cultural issues, this generation demonstrates great tolerance of alternate religions and lifestyles. With regard to homosexuality a large majority support gay rights, including the right to adopt – though they remain evenly divided on gay marriage. This suggests that even the youngest adults retain traditional views of marriage, but even here there's significant change. As for abortion, this generation reflects societal views as a whole (which are largely open), and regarding the stem-cell issue, they're not that aware yet. But given time, I expect that will change as well.

As interested as I may be in the political and cultural dimensions of this generation, my greatest interest is in their views of religion. Historically, young people are the least religious of Americans, but this cohort is even less so. Perhaps that can be explained by their parentage. Baby Boomers have been more likely to opt out than earlier generations, and so it's not surprising that their children grow up in essentially non-religious households. Still, the statistic that jumps out is the 20% who claim to have no religion or who are atheist or agnostic. That is a jump of 9 percentage points from the number given by the same age group in 1987-1988. It's also a 9% differential from those who are over 26. Interestingly, the number saying they're other – such as Muslims, Hindus, and Buddhists – has remained stable. Catholic numbers are down 4%, but Protestant numbers have dropped 8 percentage points since 1987, from 52% to 44% in this survey. Though we often hear about the growth of conservative churches, such a steep drop can't be explained simply by a continued decline in Mainline Protestantism.

One bellweather issue that may signal an important change in the nation's religious thinking concerns the creation-evolution debate. Although 46% of Baby Boomers believe in something akin to young earth creationism, this drops to 33% among Generation Next (63% affirm evolution). I think this is a significant move, and as someone who believes that evolution is compatible with the Christian faith, I find it to be a welcome one.

What will the world look like in the coming years? It's likely that things will be different. Today's winners maybe tomorrows losers, and vice versa, and while I don't expect religion to disappear, it's quite possible that we're looking at the start of a redrawing of the nation's religious map. The future will be interesting!

Answers to the Big Questions of Life

Religion is becoming an increasingly public affair. It figures strongly in political campaigns and discussions of science. Although deeply personal, religion isn't simply a private matter, because if we're deeply religious our faith will influence every aspect of our lives. As influential as it might be there is no such thing as a generic, one-size-fits-all kind of religion. Religion and spirituality address similar questions, but the answers provided are as different as the religions themselves. At times our religious offerings can be quite profound, while at other times they are extremely shallow. Just as there are expressions that are angry and violent, there are others that peaceful, gentle, and compassionate.

Whether it's organized or not, religion has not disappeared, despite advances in education, technology, and scientific discovery. Many of the questions it once addressed, no longer fit within its purview. That said, we seem drawn to religious faith because it helps us deal with questions of identity and purpose. Sometimes the answers given are flippant and shallow, and require us to challenge the authorities. Years ago, Tom Skinner, an African American evangelist and social critic, responded to the raging slogan of the day, saying, "If Jesus is the answer, then what are the questions?" That's a very good question to ask, because too often we try to provide answers before listening to the questions.

Many of us, especially if we grow up in a religious setting, accept without much thought the traditions of our faith community, even if they're shallow or self-serving. This is the attitude taken by Bree Van de Kamp in an episode of the often controversial TV show *Desperate Housewives*. Yes, that's right, *Desperate Housewives* – not the sort of place one would expect to find a sophisticated discussion of religion, but to my astonishment the writers of the show treated faith questions with a degree of seriousness I wouldn't have expected.

If you follow the show, you know that the character of Lynnette Scavo faced a series of challenges that include cancer, seeing a friend being killed by a tornado, along with significant marriage issues. Having gotten to that point in life without any significant religious training or background, she begins to wrestle with spiritual questions. As she does so, she spies the prissy Bree Van de Kamp and her new husband heading off to church. Filled with questions, she decides to go to church and looks to Bree for guidance. "Where are we going?" she asks. Once at church this uninitiated seeker, who doesn't understand protocol, does something highly unusual. Lynette stands up in the middle of the sermon and presses the preacher with a series of questions. Such behavior would be shocking in most of our congregations, and I'm sure that if someone did what she did in that scene during my sermon, it would startle me, even as it startled this preacher. The highly embarrassed Bree later assures Lynette that such behavior is inappropriate, and besides "church is a place for answers – not questions." Later in the show, the pastor makes it clear that the opposite is true – church is for questions.

The issue raised by this show, which isn't known for its wholesomeness, is our apparent contentment with a shallow spirituality that fails to wrestle with the deep issues of life. While it unmasks this superficial spirituality, it reminds us that significant numbers of people are wrestling with spiritual questions that require more than pat answers. They've heard that "Jesus is the answer" (you can substitute other religious leaders for Jesus), but they'd like to ask their question before getting the answer. They want to be taken seriously as seekers after truth.

As the show ends, Lynette and Bree are seen have a serious conversation about faith. While the closing credits roll, we see them sitting on the porch reading the bible together, wrestling with those questions that dogged Lynette. At the beginning of the conversation, Bree may have believed that church is a place for clear-cut and long-established answers, rather than deep and difficult questions, but in the end she discovers that: "Faith shouldn't be blind. You don't threaten it by asking questions, you make it stronger." Indeed! And to think that such a statement comes from the mouth of a TV character is all the more amazing!

IS IGNORANCE BLISS?

When it comes to religion is ignorance bliss? If polling numbers can be believed, a goodly number of Americans seem to believe this to be true. We may be a very religious nation, but apparently our nation's vaunted religiosity is substance-free. In great numbers we affirm our belief in God, but most of us, even those who are regular attendees, know little about the doctrinal foundations of their traditions. Boston University Religious Studies professor Stephen Prothero finds these reports to be deeply disturbing. "If," he writes, "religion is this important, we ought to know something about it, particularly in a democracy, in which political power is vested in voters (Prothero, 5)." Prothero concludes that we are a "nation of Biblical illiterates," and this can be dangerous.

It may seem insignificant that only a third of Americans know that Jesus gave the Sermon on the Mount, that a majority of Americans believe that Jesus was born in Jerusalem, or that ten percent of Americans think that Joan of Arc was Noah's wife! It would be insignificant if it was just a matter of knowing trivia, but because partisans on all sides appeal to religion, and more specifically to the Bible, in support of their positions, it because a much more important issue. For, while a wall may separate church and state, the political debates in this country are frequently framed in moral and religious terms. So, if we don't know what our traditions believe and teach on such issues as immigration, homosexuality, abortion, the environment, poverty, and immigration, how can we make informed decisions? That is, unless religion is private and has nothing to do with the way I live in public.

In recent years the Republican Party has been identified by the majority of voters as the party of moral values, while the Democratic Party is seen by many as secular and unfriendly to religion. Although in the 2008 Presidential election cycle much effort was taken to try to change that perception, it's a perception that has been difficult to change. Indeed, long after Barack Obama became President, questions were being raised about his faith perspective (large numbers of members of the opposing party insisted he was a Muslim). One of the reasons why Democrats have been more reticent to speak of faith is that in the minds of many, religion has been defined by its fundamentalist proponents, and Democrats have found this to be off-putting.

One of the reasons why religious literacy is important is that it helps us discern the difference between the teachings of one's faith tradition and the culture in which we live. It can also play an important role in helping us discern whether the positions of a political party are in line with the teachings of our faith. For example, Jesus appealed to Isaiah and claimed that his ministry was directed at "bringing good news to the poor . . . release to the captives and recovery of sight to the blind, to let the oppressed go free" (Luke 4:18). One might ask which party best reflects these concerns of Jesus? Although in recent years the word moral has largely been used in reference to issues relating to sex – abstinence education, abortion, and homosexuality – aren't issues like health care, war, torture, and poverty moral issues? If so, then isn't it appropriate to ask which party or candidate reflects best the views of one's faith tradition?

In the 2008 election cycle religion became an important issue in the political conversation, as it has again in 2012. In 2008 Barak Obama, for instance, was a member of a large black congregation affiliated with the United Church of Christ until unflattering videos emerged that featured his former pastor speaking of America in ways that offended many would be voters. His closest rival in 2008, Hillary Clinton was a United Methodist. The eventual Republican nominee, John McCain was affiliated (though not a member) with a large Baptist church, while Mike Huckabee, a GOP candidate, had been a Southern Baptist pastor, before getting involved in politics. Mitt Romney, who is running again in 2012 is a Mormon, a religious group many Christians consider cultic or, at the very least, a bit strange in its teachings and practices. Rick Santorum and Newt Gingrich are Roman Catholic, and while being

Roman Catholic is no longer an impediment to higher office, Catholic candidates have to deal with the positions the church has taken on politically charged issues, especially abortion.

Ignorance may be bliss but we live in an age when ignorance of our own faith and the faiths of others is a problem. There is need for education. The question is where to get it? Stephen Prothero has an answer to that question, but it's quite controversial. He suggests that our schools add courses in Bible and Comparative Religion to our curriculum. Critics charge that such a solution is unconstitutional, but as Prothero points out, what is unconstitutional is sectarian and devotional teaching of religion, not an objective/scholarly teaching about religion. Such instruction won't be the same as what you get in Sunday school! That of course might be a problem for others who want a stronger, more sectarian strain of religious teaching.

Religious instruction like this would take trained and objective teachers. It would also require a community that is supportive of a non-sectarian, non-devotional study of religion. Of course there's the additional problem of space in the curriculum – if you insert one thing something else will have to be jettisoned. But, if an understanding of the basic elements of religion is essential to our civic life, then perhaps we should consider such a proposal. Churches, synagogues, temples, and mosques must do a better job of teaching their faith, but that simply won't cover all the bases if we're to be a truly educated people who live in a properly ordered democracy.

VARIETIES OF FAITH,
A COMMON CAUSE?

OUT OF THE MANY, ONE

Before "In God we Trust" became our national motto, America's defining mission statement was *E Pluribus Unum* (Out of the Many, One). I trust in God, but I prefer our original national motto, because it defines our national purpose and reminds us that we're a nation diverse in ethnicity, languages, cultures, and religious identities. That we can be one people in the midst of such diversity is a bold idea that must not be taken lightly.

The question is: How shall we live together, peacefully and productively, as one people in the midst of all this diversity? Answers to this question generally fallen into two categories that can be best understood by way of analogy: Melting pot and salad bowl. The melting pot image has long been popular – through assimilation our various identities melt away to create something generically American – but a more realistic analogy might be the salad bowl. The melting pot ideal may have worked in earlier days, when most immigrants were British or Northern European, but even then there were problems, as can be seen in the legacy of slavery and the Trail of Tears.

The salad bowl analogy is more realistic, because it recognizes that our differences don't easily fade away. We may be Americans, but we're also something else – African, Italian, Asian, English, Arab, Latin American ... We're Jewish, Hindu, Buddhist, Muslim, Orthodox Christian, Catholic, Protestant, or perhaps none of the above. A good garden salad has lots of great ingredients that retain their identity even as they're tossed into the salad – tomato, green onion, spinach, baby arugula, radicchio, romaine, radish, carrot, croutons, maybe some blue cheese, and the dressing of one's choice. Each ingredient adds flavor and texture to the salad. It's true that over time assimilation does happen, but even with intermarriage and a standardized education, we remain products of our heritage and common experiences, just like a salad.

By most accounts the United States is among the most *religious* nations in the world, and we're also among the most religiously *diverse* nations. This means that peaceful coexistence requires something from us that's often proven difficult to come by. It requires an ability to honor and respect our neighbors' religious identities, even when they're quite different from our own. We needn't agree on everything, nor must we lessen our devotion to the principles of our faith, but at the very least, we must accord others the right to practice their faith in peace and in dignity.

Through conversations with people of other faiths I've discovered that they have wisdom and insights that can enhance my own faith. Their experiences remind me that most of us are seeking something that transcends our own life experience. Indeed, most of us are seeking some type of connection with the divine. Our experiences and understandings may differ and even be irreconcilable. Resurrection is quite different from Nirvana or reincarnation, and the Christian doctrine of the Trinity differs from the strict monotheism of Judaism and Islam or the monism of Buddhism. Important conversations can be had on the merits of these belief systems, but our differences needn't lead to strife and division. We needn't show disrespect or dishonor to someone whose beliefs differ from our own. Perhaps we could even recognize that God might speak through religious traditions that are quite different from our own. It's possible that we'll even discover that our own understandings and experiences are less than complete, and that God is greater than our own ability to comprehend the meaning of God's existence. In the end, perhaps the lesson to be learned in this more pluralistic age is that we should listen more and talk less!

LIVING TOGETHER – RELIGIOUS PLURALISM IN THE AMERICAN PUBLIC SQUARE

Religion is a universal attribute of human existence. Officially atheistic nations haven't rooted it out, nor have economic, scientific, or educational advances diminished its presence. Religions may resist modernity and they may adapt to it, but they persist because they seem to give meaning and purpose to life, especially in times of crisis and uncertainty.

Sociologists, psychologists, biologists, and theologians have explored religion's resilience and offer interesting ideas as to why this is true. Two Christian theologians of ages past, Augustine and John Calvin, offer similar ideas that suggest that the religious impulse is innate to human existence. Augustine wrote that humankind is restless until it finds rest in God. Calvin borrowed from Cicero and spoke of a *sensus divinitas* (sense of divinity) that indwells us all and gives rise to the spiritual journey. How this works might be a matter of debate, but it is an intriguing idea.

In spite of their ubiquity, religious traditions, even ones that are similar, offer different answers and interpretations to our spiritual questions. For some God is a personal being, while for others the divine and the material seem indistinguishable. Religious perspectives often appear to be contradictory and even mutually exclusive. Reincarnation, for instance, stands in striking contrast to resurrection, but since neither is subject to scientific validation we must decide which makes the most sense on other grounds. As different as they are, the many religious traditions have similarities. It is these similarities that make conversation possible, but it is the differences that so often cause scandal that make the conversation both difficult and interesting.

September 11, 2001 made it imperative that we pay attention to the growing religious diversity in our midst. 9-11 awakened us to a diversity that had long been ignored. Not too long ago, religious pluralism could be summed up in the phrase "Protestant, Catholic, Jew," and too often we act as if this continues to be true. Today, however, our community includes Muslims, Buddhists, Hindus, Taoists, Sikhs, Catholics, Protestants, Orthodox, Mormons, Jews, Wiccans, Baha'i, Native American religions, and more. Mosques, temples, synagogues, and shrines are now joining churches in America's town squares where Protestant Christianity once dominated. We can debate whether this is good or not, but the reality of this diversity is not up for debate.

Interfaith dialog is risky. Getting to know and to understand other perspectives and traditions may change the way we understand God, humanity, and the universe. If we take up the task we will have to balance our commitments to our own faith with the need to listen with respect and understanding to the views of others. Yet, this is the challenge of living out our national motto of *e pluribus unum* ("out of many, one").

As one who is deeply committed to the tenets of the Christian faith, I have in recent years felt compelled to engage in interfaith conversation and activity. Maybe it is a matter of curiosity, or maybe it is because I believe that our fate as a planet depends on this conversation. Secularism may reign in Europe, but religion remains a significant force throughout the rest of the world. Ignoring religious pluralism will not make it go away.

Paul Tillich wrote that "religion is, first, an open hand to receive a gift and, second, an acting hand to distribute gifts" (Tillich, Essential, 116). We have received the gift of life from God (however we understand God). If we are true to this gift, then we must share it with others. We may not, nor should we, give up our distinctive beliefs, but it is important that we make every effort to understand and respect the beliefs and practices of our neighbors. Because they are different does not make them evil nor does it make them inherently good. Hopefully our conversations will bring out the best in all of us. Though living together in peace, with all of our particularities, may be difficult, it isn't impossible.

As we consider this religion filled world of ours, may we remember that true religion is not about the self, but is instead about serving the other. If we remember this, we can learn to live together in peace, and we will find a way to heal a broken world together.

Sharing the Public Square with "Other Religions"

There are various ways of dealing with religious pluralism. One method is to declare oneself to be a religious state, favor one religion, and then grant religious freedom to other faith traditions – though these other traditions are given second class standing. Israel is a good example of this response, and something similar occurs in Russia. Other countries, such as France and Turkey, have declared themselves to be explicitly secular states and limit public expressions of religion, including the wearing of religiously linked clothing and jewelry. Then there is Great Britain, which has an established church but allows considerable freedom of religious expression to those not inclined to join with the official church. In the United States there is no established religion, so the marketplace, though dominated by Christianity, offers considerable variety.

In spite of this freedom, certain religion traditions continue to find it difficult to live out their faith traditions fully. Sikhs, for instance, face considerable obstacles due to some of their practices, including the carrying of ceremonial daggers. Jews have at times faced difficulties, though by and large they have assimilated fairly well into the American society – as seen in their presence in government, academia, and business. Mormons remain suspect because of their theology and former practices, but they too have assimilated fairly well in recent years, as seen in their considerable growth outside their Utah base, along with increased presence in Congress. This is true despite the fact that many Christians consider them to be a cult, a view that has caused problems for at least one major candidacy for the presidency.

Although there are adherents from a wide variety of faith traditions struggling to find their place in the public square, perhaps no religious group faces as many challenges at this moment as does Islam. Hindus and Buddhists remain fairly exotic to many people in this Christian dominated land, largely because the Eastern religious traditions look at reality in very different ways when compared with the Western/Abrahamic faiths. But Muslims face a daunting task because of Islamic-linked terrorism (including the remembrance of the events of 9-11-2001). In addition, Muslims must deal with the fact that America has engaged in wars in three wars involving Muslim countries, as well as the fact that a significant amount of oil used in America is imported from Muslim countries. It probably doesn't help American Muslims that despite being the world's second largest religion, with well over one billion adherents, their numbers in the US are relatively small. Unfortunately this is unlikely to change any time soon, at least as long as the United States remains dependent on oil from the Middle East and is entangled in Middle Eastern wars and upheavals.

Despite the odds, Islam seems to have found a home in the United States. At this time there are two Muslims in Congress, though both of them are African-American converts to Islam. There are popular athletes such as Muhammad Ali and Kareem Abdul Jabbar, who are also converts to Islam. Perhaps the fact that they are Muslims hasn't registered with sports-minded Americans.

The question that faces the people of faith is how to remain faithful to one's faith while sharing the public square. Perhaps the answer to this question begins with the recognition that whatever space we may be given, is shared with others. And if ours happens to be the majority faith, then it is incumbent upon us to not impose our theology and practices on others who share this square – including those who do not profess any faith at all. Now, in the marketplace of ideas, it is certainly appropriate to share one's faith with others, but always keeping in mind that these conversations should be respectful, humble, and civil. Yes, our ability to unravel this Gordian knot of increasing diversity depends on our ability to hold true to our own faith traditions while respecting the views of those with whom we differ. This will not be easy, which is why religion so often proves to be divisive rather than uniting. But this isn't an impossible dream!

So, how should we behave in the public square? I suppose, at least in the United States, where freedom of speech and expression is protected by the Constitution, I am free to wear a sandwich board and stand on a street corner preaching at everyone who goes by. I might even find biblical support for such a venture in the preaching of Jonah and Paul. But, if we're to live out our faith publicly it doesn't mean being obnoxious or offensive. It simply means that as I live out my life in the public square, my faith will guide this effort. It will influence the way I vote and behave. For me, personally, it instills in me a sense of compassion for the poor, the hurting, and the marginalized. It influences the way I view issues of the environment, education, border policy, capital punishment, and many other issues. Many Christians, whose readings of Scripture differ from mine, may take a different view from me, and some may even question my faith, but, in finding this balance, we can find ways of living peacefully, productively, and justly, in a diverse and pluralistic public square.

IS AMERICA A CHRISTIAN NATION?

Is America a Christian nation? If one means by that question: Which religion is dominant in America? Then yes, one can rightfully say that America is a predominantly Christian nation, with a decidedly Protestant cast. But that's not the way the question is usually asked. To put it more precisely, the question appears to be: "Is America a Christian nation the way Saudi Arabia is a Muslim one?" That may be putting it a bit too starkly, but the way the question is usually asked concerns the role Christianity should play in determining the cultural, legal, and political dimensions of American life. There are a great many Americans who believe that Christianity should have a privileged place in American society and that it should set the tone for American life. Others would disagree vehemently, even suggesting that religion should have no place in public life.

This debate has become increasingly bitter in recent years as the poles have become increasingly stark. In the course of these debates, there is a tendency to look to the Founding Generation for precedents. We ask such questions as: Were the Founders believers? Or, did they believe in the separation of church and state? Just as many Christians, left and right, seek to defend their own positions with biblical references, partisans left and right seek out historical proof texts that they believe will support their viewpoints. For some, George Washington is the epitome of Christian piety, while for others the Founders not only were skeptics, but even despised Christianity.

Much of what we hear and read, unfortunately, is more myth and legend than facts of history, and these myths are told and retold largely for political benefit. The truth, like America itself, is much more complex.

Fortunately there are resources that help set the story straight. Books such as Jon Meacham's *American Gospel* (Random House, 2006), David Holmes's *The Faiths of the Founding Fathers* (Oxford University Press, 2006), and more recently John Fea's *Was America*

Founded as a Christian Nation? (WJK, 2011), tell a much more nuanced story, one that recognizes the contributions of Christianity to the nation's history, but which also acknowledge other important contributors such as the Enlightenment.

A noted historian and an Episcopalian, Holmes suggests that the first five Presidents, along with Benjamin Franklin, were Christian Deists. By his definition of Christian Deist, he means that these Founders belonged to their respective Protestant Churches, but weren't orthodox in their beliefs or practices. Their God was largely disinterested in our personal daily lives, but this Creator did guide the broad currents of history (providence). They believed in life after death and revered Jesus as a teacher, but they weren't Trinitarians nor did they believe in the divinity of Jesus. Their wives and daughters, on the other hand, tended to be quite pious – the exceptions being Abigail Adams and Dolley Madison. Still, this Deism was balanced by other very orthodox expressions of Christian faith on the part of people like Samuel Adams (cousin to John), John Jay, and Patrick Henry.

Whether in their orthodoxy or in their skepticism, the Founding Generation recognized the need for religious freedom, and they also understood something that seems lost today – we can work together to accomplish great things, whether spurred on by faith or not, and our differences needn't get in the way. I'm a person of faith and my faith is the driving force in my life and in my political convictions, but I know that there are people of good faith who differ from me in their religious perspectives and their political perspectives. I should be able to work with them when and where it's appropriate.

So, is America a Christian nation? Only in the sense that Christianity is and has been the dominant form of religious expression, at least among European Americans, from the earliest days of settlement. David Holmes makes the point that contemporary American authors needn't "revise history to align the founder's beliefs with their own." Rather we must tell the story, "warts and all," for to do otherwise is to "be untrue not only to history but also to the founders themselves" (Holmes, p. 164). America is, in my mind, bigger than these attempts to manipulate our history for political gain. We will be better off if we're willing and able to hear and abide the truth of our own history.

MIXING FAITH INTO PUBLIC LIFE?

People of faith have long wrestled with the place of faith in the public square. At times religious groups have sought to dominate or control the public square. At other times, they have allowed the state/nation to dominate and control the faith community. Others have sought to distance themselves from the public square – with the Amish being the most distinct example of this. There was a time, a half century ago or more that mainline Protestantism played a significant role in the public square while evangelicals largely stepped away. In the past three decades the roles have reversed.

The question that is being raised at this time in a number of sectors has to do with whether faith should engage the public square and if so, how should this engagement occur. I have found Mark Toulouse's book *God in Public: Four Ways American Christian and Public Life Relate* (WJK Press, 2006), to be very helpful in this matter. Mark has a good sense of the relationship between religion and the public square.

In this book, Toulouse focuses on the past fifty years, a period in which the nation has moved from homogeneity (at least on a regional level) to much great diversity. We are now seeing how this plays out, as folks battle it out as to who will control America's identity. Focusing on those who would want to see faith engage with the public square, Mark lays out four options – not all of which he views in a positive vein: Iconic Faith, Priestly Faith, the Public Christian, and the Public Church. The book was written to help Christians find their place in public life, but in many ways what is true for Christians could be true for people affirming other faith traditions.

√   **Iconic Faith**
Iconic Faith is an expression of civil religion in which religious symbols become nationalized or national symbols take on a sacred hue. Thus, a religious symbol, such as the Bible, takes on a nationalistic identity. This can be seen in the way in which the Bible is used in

ceremonies such as the swearing in of a President or other official – or as the "guarantor of truth" when taking oaths in court. On the other side of things, icons such as flags take on venerated status. Thus to burn a flag is to desecrate it. In this kind of engagement the church is rather passive. It simply allows its symbols to be used for state purposes. Of course, sometimes this becomes tricky, such as when a Muslim takes the oath on the Qur'an – in contravention to tradition that privileges Christian icons.

√ **Priestly Faith**

The idea of a priestly faith is expressed most clearly in the ideology of America as a Christian nation. In this way of seeing things, America is the vehicle for God's work in the World. We are, as a nation, a chosen people, a special people, with a special calling. The church, therefore, is called upon to be the nation's priests. They give moral support to the state or the nation. America's interests and causes take on the aura of divine missions. It is expressed in ideologies such as American Exceptionalism, wherein Americans claim a certain specialness that makes them different from others, indeed makes them better than other nations, as well as in the idea of Manifest Destiny. Of course, if one is not part of the majority religion, then one is looked at with a certain degree of suspicion. People of other faiths will be tolerated, but they will not be allowed to contribute to the nation's identity.

√ **Public Christian (Public Person of Faith)**

A third style of engagement is that of the Public Christian. It is a sentiment that has a long pedigree. Although this view is rooted in Augustine's "two cities" doctrine and Martin Luther's "two kingdoms" doctrine, it is also present in Anabaptist traditions as well – though in a much different manner. In this style, the church remains an entity separate from the public sphere. One realm is spiritual and the other is earthly. Christians are encouraged to engage the public square and bring their faith perspectives into the conversation, but the church should remain separate from public debates. It is a spiritual entity not an earthly one. The church may lift up issues and cultivate a sense of social justice in the individual, but the church itself will not engage in public action, especially action that could be seen as political in nature. For those of an Anabaptist persuasion, this style goes even further, so that Christians are to refrain from participation in the public square.

√ **Public Church**

In this style of engagement, the church itself steps into the arena. It not only nurtures and cultivates people of faith who engage the public square, but it takes up the issues of the day. It becomes an advocate for social justice. The Public Church model finds its roots in John Calvin's belief that all human life stands under the Kingdom of God and Albrecht Ritschl's "Ethical Imperative." It undergirded the Social Gospel Movement (Walter Rauschenbusch) and Civil Rights Movements (Martin Luther King, Jr.). The danger that is present in this style of engagement is the difficulty in knowing where to draw the line between the church's activism and the possibility of becoming a tool of party or nation. That is, there is the possibility that the church can fall into the trap sprung by advocates of "Priestly Faith." The way in which one avoids this possibility involves great humility and great discernment. It requires that we neither absolutize our faith or our nation.

With Mark Toulouse I'm drawn to the Public Church ideal, but I also know that it's difficult to remain faithful to one's ideals when stepping into the fray. The other issue that makes this style fraught with danger is that most churches (at least Mainline Protestant churches) are not composed of people who are of one mind politically. There are many dangers to be avoided, and for this conversation to be fruitful then neither church nor party should ever feel beholden to the other. As Rabbi Arthur Gross-Schaeffer and I put it an article published in the journal *Congregations*: "Clergy must not take on the role of kingmaker or inappropriately use their influence to dictate policy" (Gross-Schaefer, 29).

As a Christian, I believe that the gospel includes a call to engage social justice. I believe that our missional activity in the world as church should lead to transformation not only of individual lives, but of society itself. But how does this take place? How do we engage society without becoming tools of either state or party?

A QUESTION OF ALLEGIANCE –
AMERICA'S CIVIL RELIGION

Whether or not there is a wall or a blurred line separating the state from the nation's dominant religious institutions, it's important to remember that religion has played and continues to play an important role in public life. Although there are a great many faith traditions present in the nation, especially as pluralism has begun to take a greater hold on our self-understanding, there remains a strong civil religion present in the nation. For some this is as it should be, and for others it is seen as detrimental both to true faith and political independence. Nonetheless there appears to be an overarching religious sentiment that gives structure to public life in certain times and places, especially during times of national tragedy.

Although not officially Christian, this civil religion shows definite signs of Christian influence – with a touch of Jewish influence thrown in for good measure. This has led some to claim that America's civil religion is Judeo-Christian rather than simply Christian. While Judaism has had an influence in American life that would seem to outsize its numbers within the nation (consider that three of nine Supreme Court Justices are Jewish), the driving force in America's civil religion remains Christianity, whose Bible includes both the Hebrew Bible (*Tanakh*) and a New Testament. Although Christians honor their Jewish inheritance, they interpret it through the lens of the New Testament. More importantly, perhaps, the nature of the Christian inheritance has been, at least until recently, greatly influenced by the nation's British roots.

Although there has been a strong religious component to American life, whether the citizens have been active in their attendance, the degree to which this religious inheritance has influenced American life and policy has ebbed and flowed over time. It is interesting to note that many of our current uses of Civil Religion, including a Pledge of Allegiance that includes the phrase "under God," date from the 1950s, a period in which public religiosity reached its height amidst a felt threat from "Godless Communism."

One of the issues that a civil religion raises concerns the possibility that one's own faith tradition can be subsumed under this civil religion. I always find it interesting to see the American flag flying over conservative Christian churches, especially since more often than not, if there is a Christian flag, it flies below the national flag. I wonder what this says about the nature of our allegiance. As a Christian who prays the Lord's Prayer, which declares: "Our Father, who art in heaven, hallowed be thy name, thy kingdom come, thy will be done on earth as it is in heaven . . ." I wonder how my national allegiance relates to my allegiance to God.[1]

Whether the wall of separation is a high and solid structure or merely a blurry line that we're supposed to respect, experience tells us that religion and state often interact with each other. Politicians invoke God with regularity, we pledge allegiance to "one nation under God," and debate school prayer and whether creationism ought to be taught in public schools. Whether this preponderance of religious conversation in our society supports the contention of many that America is one of the most religious nations lies beyond the intentions of in this book (evidence suggest that although we're more likely to claim a religious affiliation than most other industrialized nations, our attendance at religious gatherings is rather minimal). What is true, however, is that despite the contentions of some, the public square does not seem to have become naked of religion.

One way of looking at the role that faith plays in the public square is to consider the way we view the religious beliefs of our leaders. Although there isn't an established religion in this nation, there is in fact a very distinct civil religion present in America that runs deeper than the token references to "In God We Trust" on

---

1   For more on the Lord's Prayer and its call to a higher allegiance, see my *Ultimate Allegiance: The Subversive Nature of the Lord's Prayer*, (Gonzalez, FL: Energion Publications, 2010).

our coins and pledges of allegiance that include the words "one nation under God." The public role that religion plays can be seen in the way that the nation's leaders turn to it in times of grief and crisis. In many ways, at times of national trial, the President will often become a surrogate pastor to the nation, offering words of solace and encouragement.

BY THE WAY, WHAT'S YOUR RELIGION?

The Constitution declares in Article 6 that there should be no religious test for public office. Despite this word of constitutional guidance, even in this supposedly secular age, people seem to want to know exactly what their leaders believe. In the 2008 primaries questions were raised about Mitt Romney's Mormon faith. The questions have continued since as the former Massachusetts governor moved toward seeking his party's nomination in 2012. For some, the Mormon religion is sufficient cause to vote for someone else. If Romney's Mormon faith is a problem (Republican Presidential candidate John Huntsman is also Mormon, as is Senate Majority Leader, Harry Reid, a Democrat), questions have continued to be raised about President Barack Obama's faith – with significant numbers of people believing (despite frequent attempts to prove otherwise) that he is a Muslim. Apparently being a Muslim is also problematic. If being a Mormon or a Muslim is a problem, being an atheist is simply a non-starter.

So, why is it that we're so concerned about what people believe and whether they go to church? After all, large numbers of Americans don't attend church, and in fact a growing number of people describe themselves as either "none-of-the-above" or "spiritual but not religious." Indeed, you could even say that many Americans may profess faith, but are in their daily lives "practical atheists." So, why the concern about what politicians believe?

It would seem that many Americans want their leaders to be people of faith, but they're less concerned about "orthodoxy" than they are about a sense of religious grounding. This is probably why poll after poll suggests that we're uncomfortable with leaders who are atheists – to my knowledge only one member of Congress is willing to claim that moniker. Although there is latitude in religious affiliation, many Americans seem to want leaders who represent what they view as mainstream faith traditions. Thus, Mormons seem to be at a disadvantage at this point, though, as is true of Catholics, that can change. Muslims, of course, continue to face suspicion, and yet there are more Muslims in Congress than atheists (at least confessing atheists). Ours remains a relatively religious society, even if we don't join a specific faith community or attend with any regularity. Indeed, although there is an increasing number of vocal "New Atheists," such as Richard Dawkins, whose books have sold well, the atheist choir remains rather small.

Although civil religion often is rather benign, there is a danger inherent in it. That is, when we equate God and the nation. That is, when we simply assume that God blesses whatever the nation espouses. This danger was of great concern to Dietrich Bonhoeffer, who discerned within his own country a disturbing link between religion and nationalism, a link that led to many Germans baptizing the nationalist creed of the Nazis (Moses).

THE DAY CONGRESS MARKED RELIGIOUS FIRSTS

When Congress convened on January 4, 2007 it witnessed several American religious firsts, including the seating of two Buddhists and a Muslim as congressional representatives. In 1972, fifty-one senators and 43% of the House hailed from three Protestant denominations, but that's changing, especially with the most religiously diverse Congress in history. What this means is that we're witnessing the realization of America's promise as a land of freedom for people of every religious background.

Not everyone, unfortunately, is happy about this change. The election of a Muslim from Minnesota, Keith Ellison (D-MN), to Congress made news, which might not be unexpected considering that America is at war in two Muslim countries. Some Americans feel this event in our history bodes ill for the nation. When Ellison announced that he would use the Qur'an to take his oath of office, the reaction was swift and negative. Now sacred books aren't used in the official ceremony, but only in a later private and unofficial one. Still, this reaction is an expression of xenophobic tendencies that often emerge in difficult times. It is also rooted in a growing suspicion of Muslims who are seen as somehow not truly American.

Some feel that this request to use the Qur'an is an attack on American civilization as we know it. Conservative talk show host Dennis Prager wrote: "If you are incapable of taking an oath on that book, don't serve in Congress." Judge Roy Moore of Alabama believes that since "the Islamic faith rejects our God and believes that the state must mandate the worship of its own god, Allah," a Muslim can't uphold the Constitution and still be a Muslim. Of course, Moore uses quotes from a Radical Muslim, but nothing I've read so far suggests that Ellison is a radical. Another conservative group called for the passage of a Constitutional Amendment mandating the use of the Bible in such ceremonies. Then there is the perplexing call by Congressman Virgil Goode (R-VA) to restrict immigration, especially of Muslims, lest Muslims take over Congress. It should be noted that Ellison isn't an immigrant but is instead a convert.

What Prager, Moore, the AFA, and Goode are suggesting not only runs counter to the American spirit of religious freedom; it's a direct challenge to the Constitution of the United States. While the use of the Bible in official ceremonies is a long-standing tradition and a legacy of America's civil religion, requiring its use would be an unconstitutional religious test. Article Six of the Constitution says explicitly that "no religious Test shall ever be required as a Qualification to any Office or public Trust under the United States." How ironic it is that some Americans are willing to betray the Constitution to "protect" American civilization.

America is bigger than this. At the heart of our nation's governing philosophy is a commitment to freedom for all people, a commitment that's enshrined in the Constitution, and extends to one's religious practices. Forcing someone who isn't a Christian to use the sacred text of the Christian faith in an official ceremony runs counter to this commitment to religious freedom. It also makes second-class citizens of non-Christian citizens of the nation.

If we need to use a document in ceremonies such as the swearing in of a congressperson, a judge, or the President, then why not use a copy of the Constitution. After all, our elected officials aren't being entrusted with enacting biblical statutes. As far as I know, we elect them to uphold the Constitution of the United States. As important as religion and the Bible have been to the history of the nation, the Constitution and not the Bible is the unifying document in our country. Besides, it doesn't appear that using the Bible in such ceremonies is much of a guarantor of honesty or trustworthiness. Besides that, there's an inconvenient saying of Jesus forbidding the taking of oaths on anything, including Heaven. Instead, he says: let our word be "'Yes, Yes' or 'No, No'; anything more than this comes from the evil one" (Matthew 5:33-38). Despite the din of rancorous pronouncements, this is an important year in the life of our nation. So, as we mark a new chapter in America's political and religious life, I want to say congratulations to Keith Ellison and also wish him the best as he represents his district and his nation in Congress.

TALKING RELIGION IN PUBLIC

I know it's not polite to talk about religion or politics in public. Unfortunately I'm both religious and politically minded, and except for sports and music, there aren't many topics of greater interest to me than these two. More than twenty years ago Richard John Neuhaus wrote a book called *The Naked Public Square* (1984), a manifesto that challenged the alleged secularization of the public square. He contended that the religious voice, which he believes is the foundation of civic life, was no longer welcome in public, doing damage to the American way of life.

I mention Neuhaus's book, not because I want to deal with it or his arguments, but because the possibility that the public square could be naked is quite real. There are many countries that deny religion any place in the public square, and there are, of course, other nations where just one religion dominates the whole of public life. Though it often seems like there are only two alternatives, theocracy or "godless" secularism, from its earliest days the American republic has walked a third middle way. Religion has always played a significant role in American public life; this is why I decided to call this column in the *Lompoc Record* "Faith in the Public Square." I believe in the separation of church and state, but this isn't the same thing as the separation of religion and public life. The first is institutional, the second is personal. I can't separate my faith from my public life, because my faith involves everything about me, including my politics.

The problem today isn't that there are no public religious voices; the problem is that too many of them are strident and self-serving. People grieve the demise of western Christendom, as if the end of a triumphalist Constantinianism is the end of Christianity. As a follower of Jesus, I find it difficult to connect his life and teachings with a Constantinian view of the relationship between church and state. Remember Jesus died at the hands of the same Roman government that Constantine later lead. Though I reject the Constantinian view of church and state, I don't believe that you can keep your faith private. In this I'm of one mind with Neuhaus and Jim Wallis of Sojourners, though my views are much closer to those of Wallis than Neuhaus.

I began writing the column from which this book derives, which has a decided public edge to it, because I believe that religion (faith) belongs in the public square. My "moral values" and my faith professions influence the way I live and the way I vote, but I also know that my values and my professions of faith aren't shared by everyone. That's why I believe that we must share the public square with each other.

American society – especially California, where I spent much of my adult life – is quite diverse. Diana Eck's book *A New Religious America* (2001) carries a subtitle that says everything we need to know about modern America: *How a "Christian Country" Has Become the World's Most Religiously Diverse Nation.* Whereas once America's religious life could be summed up with Protestant, Catholic, and Jew, today mosques and temples of all kinds dot the landscape. In theory, everyone's voice is welcome in the public square. This maybe why America's Muslim community, unlike Europe's, hasn't become radicalized.

A civil and productive conversation about religion and politics must begin with the admission that I may not have all the truth. It'll also help if we remember that God is neither Republican nor Democrat. In fact, we need to remember that God isn't an American. I cringe when our political leaders claim that God is on our side. How do they know? After all, Osama Bin Laden believed that God was on *his* side.

WHO IS AMERICA'S GOD?

Depending on which poll you read (and trust) it appears that upwards of 90% of Americans believe in God. These are significant numbers, especially when compared to Europe. Despite state-supported churches throughout Western Europe, the continent is largely secularized. America, on the other hand, lacks a state-sponsored religion, but is almost "God-intoxicated" in comparison, at least, on the surface. Some polls and studies suggest that the United States isn't as far behind the Europeans when it comes to secularism.

We can argue about how many Americans really do believe in God, but a more important question concerns the kind of God Americans believe in. The answer(s) isn't a monolithic one. We may believe in a higher power, but we embrace a broad spectrum of definitions.

You could try to discern the nature of America's God by checking the yellow pages, but this could prove misleading. Reading the Yellow Pages would lead you to conclude that most "believing" Americans belong to one of the many Christian denominations, but using this criterion might cause you to leave out a growing portion of the American population that has embraced a non-institutionalized and often undefined deity. Even if we're religious on Sundays, many of us are practical atheists the rest of the week. That is, many Americans either ignore God or don't think God is very interested in their daily lives. We may turn to God in times of crisis, but when things are going okay we'd rather go it alone. So, while few of us are true atheists, many are functional atheists.

A Baylor University study entitled "American Piety in the 21st Century" provided us with a unique look at America's theologies. It not only confirms that Americans believe in God, but it also offers significant details about the god(s) we embrace. Although a plurality of Americans embraces Christianity, there are significant differences even among Christians. In fact, there are four distinct views of God that cross religious and denominational lines. The definitions relate to our perception of God's engagement with creation and God's anger.

The most popular God among Americans, with 31% of the vote, is the Authoritarian God. This God is definitely engaged in our lives, but "he" is also angry and in control. Smaller numbers of us embrace a Benevolent God (23%). This deity is also engaged but not as prone to anger as the Authoritarian God. At the other end of the spectrum are the gods who remain aloof from human experience. The Critical God (16%), for example, is angry with us, but is inclined to postpone justice until the next life. And then there's the Distant God who is almost as popular as the authoritarian one (24% of the vote). I can see why many people find this God appealing. This deity could be benevolent and yet is likely to leave us alone so we can do our own thing.

Women prefer an engaged divinity, with a slight preference for the Authoritarian God, while men prefer deities who are either detached or authoritarian. The male predisposition toward the Distant or Critical God may help explain why fewer men than women belong to religious groups. What surprised me was that younger people (18-30) are more likely to prefer an authoritarian God than do older people. Middle-aged folk like me seem to prefer a Benevolent God. Coastal dwellers like non-engaged deities, while Southerners vote overwhelmingly for an Authoritarian God. This may sound like Red State/Blue State politics, but the reality is that even within ethnic, gender, or geographic groups, there is little unanimity.

When it comes to religious identification, Evangelicals, biblical literalists, and African-American Protestants go for the authoritarian God, while a plurality of Jews, Mainline Protestants and Catholics choose the distant one. And not surprisingly, the more you pray or attend religious services the more likely you are to prefer an authoritarian deity.

Because I'm interested in the relationship between religion and public life, I was intrigued by the political implications of these four theologies. Apparently, the more we pray, read the Bible literally, or go to services, the more conservative we are politically, and the more likely we are to support increased military spending, harsh punishment of criminals, funding of faith-based organizations, and prayer in school. The more we embrace a benevolent or distant God, the more likely we are to oppose the death penalty, support business regulation, and be concerned about protecting the environment. Again this is all a matter of degree, but it does suggest that what we believe about God influences our behavior and our political convictions. This is assuming that we're one of the 90% who believes in God.

WHAT KIND OF FAITH!?

Jesus' parable of the "Widow and the Unjust Judge" ends with the question, "when the Son of Man comes, will he find faith on earth?" (Luke 18:8 NRSV). I think there's a follow up question that could be asked: "What kind of faith would he find on earth when he returns?" If you listen to critics such as Richard Dawkins and the late Christopher Hitchens, it would seem that the only kind of faith one should expect to find on earth is one that's narrow-minded, unintelligent, and dangerous. Now, there may be a degree of truth to the observation – there is indeed much narrowness, anti-intellectualism and proneness toward violence among the world's religions, including my own. These observations and critiques aren't new or unique, they're just a bit more uncompromising and even hostile.

Perhaps it's because I don't see myself in these critiques of religion offered by the so-called "New Atheists," but I do think there is something in between no religion and narrow/violent religion. In fact, the vast majority of religious people aren't prone to violence, even if many are very conservative in their thinking. The "New Atheists" often accuse moderate and liberal religionists of providing intellectual cover for narrow fundamentalism, but I would disagree (obviously). It's simply that this voice hasn't gotten much press of late – indeed the press seems to prefer the extremes to a more reasoned and centrist position.

But there are signs out there that many people are interested in more open-minded and positive religious expressions. These can be progressive or liberal, but they don't have to be. It's not so much the content as it is the attitude that's important.

In the book *Asphalt Jesus,* written by a fairly liberal pastor named Eric Elnes we read the story of a journey on foot that took Elnes and five other walkers, together with a support team, across the country. This small group of progressive Christians walked from Phoenix to Washington, DC, bearing witness to the principles set down in the *Phoenix Affirmations.* The *Affirmations* is a brief statement of progressive Christian principles that embrace openness to God's presence in other traditions, affirms the equality of all people no matter their race, ethnicity, gender, age, or sexual orientation, and calls Christians to a life of prayer and service. Along their journey – on foot – they encountered, often in unexpected places, people of faith who were full of warmth, inquisitiveness, and welcome. They also experienced rejection and hostility – more often from fellow Christians than from non-Christians. Elnes writes of his surprise at finding so many people open to conversation, people seeking to hear alternative voices. What they discovered is that you don't have to agree with each other to love each other.

As I read the book I resonated with his descriptions of people seeking a positive and compassionate spirituality, a Christianity that was committed to making the world a better place to live in. My sense is that there are lots of people, many of whom may feel disconnected from institutionalized religion, who are spiritually hungry and looking for a safe home, a place where they can share their doubts, questions, and concerns. They want a faith that's committed to public service, but they're tired of polarizing and politicized forms of religion. Indeed, they want an experience with God that will make a difference in their lives and in the lives of their children and their grandchildren. They may feel like they're alone, and yet as Eric Elnes discovered, there are many others who feel exactly the same way. Some are conservative, others are liberal. Many are somewhere in between. Now the time has come for those of us who are committed to a new way of being faithful to speak up.

I find a way forward in this statement from the *Phoenix Affirmations*. Speaking as a Christian, I hear the call to love our neighbors by "walking humbly with God, acknowledging our own shortcomings while honestly seeking to understand and call forth the best in others, including those who consider us their enemies." If we would do just this one thing, the world would indeed be a better place.

BLESSING THE NATIONS – A COMMON CAUSE FOR ABRAHAM'S CHILDREN?

Danish cartoons lampooning Muhammad give rise to deadly riots; the Iranian president announces a contest to disprove the Holocaust – just a few examples of a lingering and violent family feud. Muslim, Jew, and Christian are, at least symbolically, children of Abraham. Yet, these children of Abraham's are major contributors to the wars, violence, hatred, mistrust, suspicion, and intolerance that tear at the social fabric of our world.

Abraham is the patriarch from whom Jews, Christians, and Muslims claim descent. They are cousins who have too often become bitter rivals. Though the biblical story is full of such rivalries – Cain and Abel, Isaac and Ishmael, Jacob and Esau – these rivalries need not go on forever. There are also stories in scripture of family reconciliation.

Genesis tells of God's covenant with Abraham and the commission to bless the nations. Though the Qur'an states it differently, the idea is present within its pages (Surah 2:124-125). Each faith tradition sees itself as a conduit of blessing, but each finds it difficult to acknowledge the other's calling. But by listening to each other's stories we may discover a common cause. If we put aside our anger, fear, and suspicion, we may find it possible to move beyond mere toleration to finding ways of blessing humanity, whom we each believe is created in the image of God. Indeed, if we examine carefully the scriptures of each faith, we find that this is specifically what we are called to do.

Bruce Feiler's book, *Abraham*, offers an inspiring and instructive vision of how Abraham could be a source of unity, though I was recently reminded that Abraham's story has very different meanings for each tradition. We may revere Abraham, but we also convert him to our own cause. This makes the conversation more difficult, but not impossible. It is worth remembering that for one Abraham is the follower of Torah before there was a Torah, for another he is the paradigm of faith in one not yet born, and for the third he is one who submits. He is Jew, Christian and Muslim, and yet he is none of them.

Still, in Abraham, each tradition draws inspiration and guidance. So, in a sense he remains our common father. In his offspring with Hagar and Sarah, the nations are to be blessed, which makes it imperative that we listen to each other instead of perpetuating the kind of mistrust that leads to violence.

Crusades, pogroms, jihads, genocide and holocaust, together with the ongoing conflict between Israeli and Palestinian are expressions of our inability to hear Abraham's voice calling us to be a blessing. The war torn Holy Land is a reminder of a common story that at least for Jews and Christians begins with Abraham's journey to Canaan. It continues with a return under Moses of the children of Israel to the Promised Land. It is there that a Temple is built, destroyed, and rebuilt, and then destroyed. It is on its roads that Jesus walked, teaching the ways of God before dying on a Roman cross outside Jerusalem's walls. Here Muhammad received the Qur'an and ascended into heaven. Three religions lay claim to this holy land but are unable to share it peacefully. We are truly a dysfunctional family, but it isn't too late for the family to begin talking. The answer to the violence can be found in our recognition of the family resemblance, and in our recognition that as members of the human family we are all created in the image of the God.

We may tell different stories about our ancestor, but by listening to each other's stories we will learn of a common cause – a call to bless humanity. Before we start talking it might help to do some family research. According to Genesis, when Abraham was dying, his two estranged sons came together to bury their father. Each son received a blessing and commission from their father, who promised that they would be the fathers of many nations. The best way to honor Abraham's memory may be for those of us who share this common ancestry to join the two brothers in a pilgrimage of reconciliation and peace which would bless all of humanity.

THE DILEMMA THAT IS DECEMBER

December poses a dilemma for some, though this may come as a surprise to many. I find December to be a joyous and blessed season. I may complain occasionally about the commercialization of Christmas, but I still enjoy the lights, the trees, and the music, especially the carols. I really have no complaints.

Christmas celebrates the birth of Jesus and it reminds me that God has drawn near to us in a baby born in a far off corner of the world. It is a festival that carries a message of peace and good will, of angel's songs and divine visits. Yes, for me, "Jesus is the reason for the season."

As joyous as December is for me, I know that Jesus is not the reason for the season for all. There are those in our community whose history includes stories of persecution and even death at the hands of those who claim the name of Jesus. There are memories of exclusion and marginalization, especially among those who went through public schools in an earlier age. For Jews, Muslims, Buddhists, Hindus, Baha'is, and people of no religion, December isn't necessarily a moment of joy. Simply throwing a Hanukkah song into a mix of explicitly religious Christmas carols only seems to make the discomfort more obvious. Putting Rudolph in the crèche on the court house lawn does not make the crèche any less religious and therefore appropriate for a public square shared by all.

My Jewish friends have helped me understand how painful December can be. Yes, Jews celebrate Hanukkah during December, but this festival does not receive the same attention as Christmas, nor does it play the role in Judaism as Christmas does in Christianity. It is difficult to put on the shoes of the other person, but we who comprise the "majority" religious culture need to recognize the possibilities for exclusion. It is easy to say, well that's the way it is, so get over it. Such sentiment is neither compassionate nor in keeping with the message of peace and good will that Christmas is supposed to represent.

I have no intention of abandoning my celebration of Christmas – it is too important to my faith. I draw comfort from its promise that God came to dwell among us in the person of Jesus. I believe I am a better person because of the ways of God that are revealed in the person and teachings of Jesus. But then I am a Christian and that is how it should be.

Christianity remains the dominant religious movement in the United States and so it will be nigh impossible for Christmas, including its religious foundations, not to impact the month of December. That being said, it is possible for Christians to be sensitive to those who do not share this religion. We who are Christians can also take the opportunity to learn about the celebrations and festivals of our neighbors – from Yom Kippur to Ramadan, to Kwanzaa and beyond. By doing this we not only show sensitivity, we offer respect to those who are different.

If we who are Christian have allowed Jesus to be crowded out of Christmas, then we should make every effort to reclaim him as the reason for our celebration. We can make it a point to attend Christmas Eve and Christmas Day services. There we will sing the great carols of Christmas and we will celebrate the wondrous message of salvation and grace that is present in Christmas. At the same time, as a Christian, I hope that I will show my neighbor the respect I would want shown to me. If Christmas is about peace and good will (Luke 2:14), then it is incumbent on we who are Christians to live accordingly. If the greeting is happy holiday instead of merry Christmas, I know what is meant, and by showing respect and honor to those who do not share my religious faith I can offer a worthy gift to our community. The public square need not be naked, but it needs to be shared by all.

IS RELIGION BAD FOR THE UNIVERSE?

I consider myself to be a pretty decent person. As for my religious proclivities, I can't find anything in my life and theology that's particularly dangerous. As a pastor of a Mainline Protestant church I try to present to the world a faith that is welcoming, generous, gracious, and that seeks the transformation of the world.

When I think of bad religion I usually have someone like Osama Bin Laden and Fred Phelps in mind; on the other hand, I expect that they might say the same thing about me. So, maybe it's really a matter of perspective.

We religious people want to believe that our religion is good, and we're not always sure about anyone else's. Maybe this is why I find Sam Harris' bestseller, *Letter to a Christian Nation* (Knopf, 2006) so disconcerting. Harris is, if you don't know already, a very vocal atheist. In his mind religion may have had some evolutionary value, but whatever benefit human evolution may have gained from it is outweighed by its downside. In his words: "That religion may have served some necessary function for us in the past does not preclude the possibility that it is now the greatest impediment to our building a global civilization." Yes, our continued insistence on raising our children to be Christians, Muslims, or Jewish, needs to be recognized as "the ludicrous obscenity that it is."

Now, as I read this brief, even breezy, diatribe against religion – one that places special emphasis on the dangers posed by Christianity and Islam – I didn't recognize myself. That shouldn't surprise me, says, Harris, because he's not talking to me. His conversation partner is the "true Christian," the Fundamentalist who takes every word of Scripture with absolute literalness. I could take comfort in the fact that I don't recognize myself in his depiction of Christianity, except that he has effectively excommunicated moderate and liberal Christians like me from the Christian community.

Harris's problem with religious moderates and liberals is that they, in his estimation, give cover for "true believers." These are religious folks who are so convinced they're right in their beliefs that they'll choose violence, if necessary, to further their aims. Of course, he has plenty of historical ammunition: the Crusades, the Inquisition, the Salem witch trials, among others to choose from. Since religion is essentially irredeemable, Harris concludes that the only solution is the eradication of religion. Whatever redeeming qualities religion might possess they are far outweighed by the damage it does to human society.

If I'm honest, I must grant him the dark side of religious history, but is religion all bad? I'd suggest that one could easily argue the other side and demonstrate that people of faith have been a blessing to society. They've given more to it than they've taken from it. Hospitals, schools, orphanages, homes for the elderly, builders of homes for the poor, and more, are provided by religious communities. Though one needn't be religious to engage in such actions on behalf of society, religious people have generally been in the forefront of efforts at social change. Besides, one could easily point to Maoist and Stalinist attempts at creating a religionless society as counter examples.

Although I don't find Harris' arguments compelling enough to consider abandoning my faith, his challenge is worth looking at. That this book, as well as that of biologist Richard Dawkins, is a bestseller should warn us not to take too much comfort in the extraordinary number of Americans who supposedly believe in God. Obviously, there are great numbers of people out there who are disenchanted with the existing religious options. Additionally, he's within his rights to challenge the anti-intellectualism that can be found in many religious communities.

Sometimes we need to pay close attention to our harshest critics, because in their challenge we may find words of wisdom, even if they're unintended. Harris finds hope in the possibility that religion might be eradicated. The resurgence of religion in China, Russia, and other formerly communist nations suggest that religion isn't headed to the dustbin of history just yet. But peace in the world does require a moderate tone and a commitment to respectful conversation between people of every religion. Then, perhaps, the negatives of religion will be far outweighed by the positives.

LIVING WITH GOD AND NEIGHBOR: RECLAIMING THE TEN COMMANDMENTS

Roy Moore, a former Chief Justice of the Alabama Supreme Court, ran for Governor of Alabama on a platform to restore God and the Ten Commandments to their "rightful" place in American society. You may remember Judge Moore's attempt to place a monument to the Commandments in the rotunda of the state's courthouse. He fought orders for its removal all the way to the United States Supreme Court, which reaffirmed the ruling of the lower courts that it must be removed. Moore himself was then removed from office for his defiance, but not before he became something of a folk hero to great numbers of people across the country.

I'm all for the Ten Commandments, but I worry that they have become a political symbol to be worn on judges' robes and enshrined in marble monuments on public property. It is beyond doubt that the Ten Commandments and other biblical legal codes have influenced the development of Western legal traditions and systems. It's also true that they speak to issues of morality. But is this all that they are?

So much of the talk about the Commandments focuses on morality, but that's not their primary focus. These Commandments define the basis of a relationship between the God of Abraham, Isaac, and Jacob and a specific group of people. This people had left behind a life of slavery to live in a covenant relationship with their God (Exodus 20:1-17; Deuteronomy 5:1-21). Therefore, the Ten Commandments are less a legal or moral code than they are an agreement between two parties to live together in a covenant relationship. It is because this code is so religious that the debate has become so intense. In order for the public display of the commandments to pass constitutional muster, defenders must either advocate the breaching of the wall separating church and state or they must downplay the religious dimension of the laws. To do the latter is to violate their purpose; to do the former is to undermine constitutional protections of both church and state.

The Ten Commandments begin with several statements that define a person's relationship with God. There are prohibitions against serving other gods, making idols, and bowing to idols (some religious traditions take this to mean refraining from saying the pledge of allegiance and voting). There is also one about not taking the Lord's name in vain, which means more than not using profane language. The law concerning keeping the Sabbath is also very much a religious statement, although it is a directive rarely followed even by the most religious of us (at least in the broader Christian community). With few exceptions, Christians worship on Sunday, but the Sabbath runs from sundown Friday to sundown Saturday. So, no matter how you count them, the Ten Commandments are religious in intent and content. The final six (or final seven, depending on how you count them) deal with human relationships, but the commands are rooted in a primary relationship with God.

The best interpretation of the intent of these laws can be found in their summary, which calls on God's people to love God with the entirety of their being, and then to love their neighbors as they love themselves (Deuteronomy 6:4). In light of this summary, you could say that the way we treat our neighbor is an outgrowth of the way we view God.

I don't dispute the value of keeping the Ten Commandments; I just want to make sure we don't secularize them or make them a political shibboleth. Treating them as simply a legal code demeans them and rips them from their context as the foundation of a covenant relationship with God. Using them as part of a political platform not only demeans the Commandments, but it demeans God.

Instead of fighting over how and when to display the laws in the public square, perhaps we all should commit ourselves more earnestly to looking out for the best interests of our neighbors. If we are religious, especially if we are part of the Jewish and Christian communities, then let us seek to live out our relationship with God in a way that honors God and honors our neighbors. That will be public display enough.

Politics, Ideology, and Faith

GOD AND POLITICS ON ELECTION DAY

Election Day is a time when Americans can celebrate hard earned freedoms through the act of voting. The right to vote allows us to express our political will – a right that's still not widespread in the world.

By day's end we may have filled numerous federal, state, and local offices and decided a lengthy list of initiatives. Sadly, most Americans won't vote, some out of principle, but most do so out of apathy or disillusionment. While this sentiment is understandable, given the nastiness of many campaigns, it's disheartening and it ultimately undermines our democracy.

As has been the case in recent elections, religion plays a significant role in the political debate. Although many Americans believe that religion and politics don't mix, many others can't seem to distinguish them, and so the debate goes on. While history suggests that theocracies don't work very well, and though an Iran-style theocracy isn't in America's future, religion can and does affect elections. Religion's effect can be good and not so good.

I consider it both a civic duty and a sacred obligation to vote. Therefore, when I approach the polls, I do so as a person of faith. But, while my faith influences my voting practice, I try to keep in mind the pluralistic nature of the larger community. Others go to the polls with different faith commitments. I must, then, humbly admit that I'm not in a position to know beyond a reasonable doubt what's best for the nation. I must give room for the checks and balances of my fellow citizens' votes.

My Christian faith is a significant factor in my decision making, but I must admit that my scriptures don't always speak clearly to every political issue of the day. The Hebrew Scriptures often speak of a theocratic ideal and tell the story of a largely ineffective monarchy. The teachings of Jesus and Paul are important, but they often don't speak directly to modern life, and neither of them voted in an election. Romans 13 is the most specific statement on politics, but it was written in the context of a totalitarian regime. When you read this passage it appears that Paul's advice is to keep your head down and obey the law. But what happens when, as in a democracy, you are the ultimate source of the laws we are to obey? Can you simply keep your head down, or do you have a responsibility to be engaged in the system, as messy as it may be?

The major religions of the world differ as to the relationship between religion and politics. For some, religion should support the government, while others believe that it should be an outside critic. Muhammad was both a religious teacher and ruler, as was Moses. Jesus, however, was an itinerant preacher who often said politically provocative things. Buddha withdrew from the ruling elite, but the Dalai Lama is both ruler and teacher.

Besides all of these differences, most religions transcend national boundaries, a fact that raises questions of loyalty. Do my loyalties belong with my country or my co-religionists? If my loyalties transcend national borders, then the same is likely true of Muslims, Buddhists, Jews, Hindus, and others, unless of course I worship a national deity – which I don't.

Our coins say, "In God We Trust," but in whose God do we trust? I'm proud to be an American, but as a Christian, my first loyalty is to God. But then the same is true for others who go to the polls with God having first call on their lives. Recognizing that others will join me in voting while listening for the divine voice, I must listen carefully and critically. And if I understand God's calling, then my attention should be given to the welfare of the whole – both my fellow American citizens and my fellow citizens of the world.

As a religious person I admit that I have dual loyalties. I hope that by recognizing this, I'm better able to keep things in perspective and can grant my fellow citizens the same rights and responsibilities. While the IRS tells me that as a pastor I can't engage in partisan politics from the pulpit, I do believe I have a responsibility to speak to the important issues of the day from a faith perspective. Believing that voting is a national duty, I always encourage people to vote. I do this, however, hoping that the conscience of the voter is marked by compassion and committed to the well-being of all creation, whether American or not.

FREEDOM, RESPONSIBILITY, AND INDEPENDENCE DAY

Every year, on the fourth day of July, Independence Day makes itself felt in the United States. It is a reminder that the United States was founded on the principles of liberty and happiness for all – at least in theory. In point of fact, we've not always lived up to our ideals, but in principle we are a people committed to equal justice and opportunity. These commitments are enshrined in the words of our founding documents. The *Declaration of Independence* insists that "Governments are instituted among Men, deriving their just powers from the consent of the governed."

These freedoms have at times been abridged and set aside in the name of security or the defense of the nation, and often we've come to regret those decisions. Living as we do at a time when the government has taken steps to limit certain civil rights and freedoms, questions have been raised about the usefulness and constitutionality of these actions. Threatened from outside, or so we believe, we've allowed at least some of our freedoms to erode.

The Declaration of Independence insists that the government serves at the pleasure of the people, but at times the executive branch has taken on imperial tendencies – though the degree to which this is true may depend on who is President of the United States. (When I first wrote this essay for the *Lompoc Record* George W. Bush was President and I was less tolerant of his efforts to expand executive power than perhaps I am today when I'm more in tune with the person who is currently holding that office.) But, it's worth considering the implications of an expansion of power undertaken in the name of security. How much is too much? What liberties are being lost and will we be able to reclaim them once their gone?

Consider for a moment the claim made by our former President that he had the authority to designate citizens and foreign nationals as "enemy combatants," thereby placing them beyond normal constitutional protections (President Obama has not really backed off this claim either). I agree with John Whitehead of the

Rutherford Institute that this is possibly a dangerous and unconstitutional act.

> In a world where the president has the power to label anyone, whether a citizen or permanent resident, an enemy combatant and detain that person indefinitely without trial, no liberty exists and everyone is potentially an 'enemy combatant'.

This isn't a matter of partisan politics (from what I know of John Whitehead – he's a conservative); it's about protecting our liberties as a people – no matter who the President is. The problem is that the then President seemed especially concerned with claiming power for himself, and again the current President has not let go of these prerogatives.

Now, to claim that we are a free people doesn't mean that there are no limits to our freedoms – for instance I'm not sure if the Second Amendment really does allow anyone and everyone to walk around with an automatic weapon. The constitutional question concerns how limits are constructed and imposed.

While the Constitution and not the Declaration of Independence defines the nature of our government, the Declaration does suggest that that "we the people" – not the Executive, Congress, or the Courts – ultimately decide what the government should look like. One of the principles that the both the Constitution and the Declaration of Independence established was that government is accountable to the people. Thus, the nation's rules and regulations that are imposed by government should protect not the elite but the people as a whole. Thus, traffic and environmental laws and bans on smoking in public buildings are appropriate because they protect and serve the common good.

To temper our desire for freedom as well as give some religious input, it's appropriate to consider the words of St. Paul who suggested that while freedom is great, it's not always beneficial (1 Corinthians 10:23). Anarchy is freedom, but it usually ends with chaos and destruction. Because we often think of freedom in individualistic terms – "I can do what I want, when I want" – we often forget how our lives intersect. As Rabbi Jonathan Sacks writes: "With freedom is born responsibility." And this goes both ways – without freedom we can't be held responsible and without a sense of responsibility freedom leads to unfortunate ends – if not for me then for my neighbor.

When I think of the freedoms guaranteed by the Constitution, I think of my right to speak my mind, publish my thoughts, worship as I please, assemble when and where I wish, and petition the governing authorities. These First Amendment rights should be treasured and protected, but even here there are limits, for I must remember that my freedoms must be balanced by those of my neighbor. This concern for the needs of the other brings us back to the overarching principle enshrined in the commandment to love one's neighbor as one's self. Whether self-imposed or not, limits must be motivated by a concern for the common good.

Our Founders understood the need for checks and balances. Although they were, in general, optimistic people who trusted the People to make wise decisions, they also understood the ever-present potential for the powerful to abuse the power entrusted to them. This was why they preferred decentralized government. I'm no "Tea-Partier" and I do believe in a robust Federal Government, but when power is entrusted to the hands of a few, whether government or corporate hands, it would be appropriate to remember our calling to balance freedom and responsibility – even on the Fourth of July!

WHAT WALL OF SEPARATION?

The First Amendment grants Americans the right to freely exercise their religious preferences and prohibits government establishment of religion. Unique at the time, it's become a model of religious liberty for the world. Recently, however, our interpretation and application of the First Amendment has inspired much debate. History shows that we've never been consistent in our interpretations and practices. Though most American children no longer pray or read the Bible devotionally in school, we still have congressional and military chaplains and pledge allegiance to "one nation under God." The words "in God we trust" are imprinted on our currency and Protestantism has long appeared to have a quasi establishment as the national faith. Whatever the nature of the alleged wall of separation between church and state, it appears that the wall is quite porous.

It's true, as many are quick to point out, the Constitution doesn't mention a wall of separation, but, as others rightly point out, Thomas Jefferson's response to the Danbury Baptist Association of Connecticut (January 1802) does speak of such a wall. The Danbury Baptists sought clarification from the President, because they weren't experiencing the promised religious freedoms in Congregationalist dominated New England. Jefferson responded that the First Amendment had erected "a wall of separation between Church & State," and that "religion is a matter which lies solely between Man & his God, that he owes account to none other for his faith or his worship, that the legitimate powers of government reach actions only, & not opinions."

While the phrase "wall of separation" doesn't appear in the Constitution, it's clear that Jefferson and others among the Founders believed that the First Amendment had erected a barrier of sorts between church and state. Jefferson's close friend, James Madison, was the primary author of the Constitution, and he wrote in his "Memorial and Remonstrance against Religious Assessments," that each person has the inalienable right to exercise their religion as "conviction and conscience" directs. Regarding the establishment of religion, Madison asked: "Who does not see that the same authority which can establish Christianity, in exclusion of all other Religions, may establish with the same ease any particular sect of Christians, in exclusion of all other Sects?"

Jefferson and Madison assumed that the Constitution created a barrier separating religion and government, but they also believed that both religion and the government would benefit from this wall of separation. History has shown that their understanding of the church-state relationship is correct, no matter how porous the wall has proven to be. Even with this wall in place, however, religion continues to have a place in the public square. Witness how politicians from Jefferson and Madison and on to Barack Obama have invoked Providence and God in speeches and writings; at the same time, religious leaders from Henry Ward Beecher to Martin Luther King have stood in the public square and offered a prophetic voice on the issues of the day from the abolition of slavery to civil rights.

Although there are those who believe that Jefferson's wall is impermeable, effectively eliminating every religious voice from public life, this doesn't appear to be the intent of the First Amendment. While courts and legislatures will likely continue wrestling with the interpretation and application of the First Amendment, their rulings neither should inappropriately favor religion nor should they exclude religion from the public sphere.

When we talk about separation of church and state the central issue concerns coercion. Establishment is by its very nature coercive even when accompanied by edicts of toleration. Our problem today is that we're not sure when religion becomes coercive. An incident at the Air Force Academy, a few years back, is illustrative. It appears that school officials inappropriately interjected religion into the life of the school by encouraging the evangelization/proselytization of cadets by Evangelical Christians – using their positions in ways that proved coercive. School sponsored prayers and devotional bible reading can also be coercive, while a student-sponsored religious club that gathers to read the Qur'an or the Bible shouldn't be, as long as all religions are treated equally. Other points of contention, like the phrase "under God," are harder to get a handle on.

Ultimately, the key to resolving the debate is learning how to share the public square with dignity, civility, and respect. If we can do this, then we will have lived out the core values of our nation.

Forgiveness: the Foundation of Civic Life

In a perfect world there would be no need for forgiveness. Reality, however, demands it, at least if we're going to live in peace with each other. People have dreamed utopian dreams of a world that's egalitarian, harmonious, and peaceful. While this is an attractive dream, especially at a time when conflict rages around us, history isn't optimistic about its chances

There was a time when the boundless possibilities of the American frontier inspired such dreamers, but most of these ventures were small in scope and short in duration. The idea is good, but in practice it doesn't seem to work out as planned, and those who dream big utopian dreams, like Mao and Pol Pot, usually fall prey to totalitarianism.

If utopianism is merely a dream with nightmarish consequences, what are the alternatives? One "realistic" alternative with a long historical pedigree is the principle of an "eye for an eye." If you hurt me or my family, I'll hurt you and your family. Attack my country, we'll attack yours. Such tit-for-tat solutions only lead to ongoing cycles of violence and destruction.

There is a third way. It might not seem realistic, but it's the only alternative that offers the hope of reconciliation and peace in a less than perfect world. This is the path of forgiveness, a path that recognizes the humanity's imperfections but also offers the hope of a new beginning. In a zero tolerance age, forgiveness isn't always a popular notion, but when you consider the alternatives, is there any other way to go?

It's important to remember that forgiveness has a partner called justice. Justice is important, because it reminds us of the need for accountability and responsibility. Unfortunately, it's not easy to hold justice and forgiveness together, but a lasting solution to the world's problems requires that they be kept together.

Forgiveness seems to be a message found in most religions, and Jesus told his disciple Peter that we should forgive an offender not just seven times, but seventy times seven (Matthew 18:21-22). In other words, forgive until you can't keep track of the offenses. As hard as it is to hear such a word, is there any other way to get beyond the endless cycles of blame, hatred, and violence. To forgive doesn't mean that offenders aren't held accountable for their actions, but forgiveness does offer the hope of a new beginning and it sets aside the need to get revenge.

Consider for a moment the immigration debate. Critics of the now dead and admittedly less than perfect Senate immigration bill charged its sponsors with offering "blanket amnesty" to illegals. But as I read it, it tries to balance accountability with forgiveness. It sought to reduce incentives for immigration while recognizing the facts on the ground. You can criminalize immigrants, or you can find a way for them to become citizens. To me, that sounds just and forgiving, which is really a humane solution.

Forgiveness isn't easy, because it forces us to face the truth about ourselves and about our neighbors. Consider the efforts taken in South Africa to bring black and white together to build an integrated and peaceful society. The results aren't perfect, but the principle behind this effort brings together truth telling and forgiveness. Compare for a moment South Africa and Zimbabwe. One nation has experienced unimagined stability, while the other remains in chaos. South Africa took the path of forgiveness, Zimbabwe didn't.

Fred Craddock, a preacher from my denomination, wrote that "there can be no forgiveness without standards and values being violated, without persons and relationships being hurt, without a loss so deeply felt that efforts at restoration are pursued." The willingness to forgive and start again is the key to a peaceful future. That in itself may seem utopian, but the weapons of today make the wars of tomorrow an apocalyptic nightmare. The hope of our world requires that we pursue the path of forgiveness. It's a path that begins with my making the first move; if I wait for you, I may wait forever. If we're going to construct a society that is just and harmonious, a society that isn't polarized and marred by violence, then we must begin by embracing the divine call to forgive one another.

DEMOCRACY'S DARKER SIDE

I believe in democracy because despite its messiness it's the best political system yet devised. In theory, it empowers us to take control of our lives, but if it's to work we must take responsibility for our lives and actions. Freedom and responsibility are the two sides of the democracy, and an effective democracy requires that these two be kept in balance. Or, as St. Paul said: "'All things are lawful for me', but not all things are beneficial" (1 Corinthians 6:12).

Democracy is the one system of government that offers citizens the opportunity to join in governance. Even if the process is confusing and at times inane, we get to choose our leaders. Often the political process seems to continue on without end, with one election cycle giving way to the next. Disenchantment with the two major political parties has led many Americans to describe themselves as Independents, though it's unlikely that a third party candidate will become President anytime soon (the last time a new party emerged that had a chance at achieving that goal was the 1850s when the Republicans replaced the Whigs). These Independents live up to their moniker, making them difficult to classify. But, now that neither party controls a majority of votes in the nation's elections, they have the opportunity to sway elections. All of this makes for a messy democratic process.

Despite the benefits of democracy, it can have a dark side. This dark side is rooted in the fact that we must we must entrust our lives – as the electorate – to the whims of our fellow citizens. We who vote are fallible women and men, and the people we choose to represent us are equally fallible. It's interesting that despite the cries of the citizenry about a corrupt and unresponsive government, we tend to be pleased with those who represent us. It's the other person's choice who is the problem.

We see this dark side in the way we go about choosing a candidate. Effective democracy, especially in its purest forms, requires a diligent and informed electorate. Voters need to have the time, the education, and the inclination, to look into the issues, as well as the backgrounds, values and views of the candidates.

In real life, numerous factors influence our choices, some of which may be less than honorable. It could be the way a candidate speaks or looks. We may take into consideration a candidate's gender, race, or age. Fear is a potent influence – and candidates and parties are very adept at manipulating them. Then there are the promises candidates make, promises that often pander to our prejudices or sense of entitlement. Too often we vote our own self-interest at the expense of our neighbors. That is, altruism often takes a back seat to me-first-ism. We may voice our support for the biblical premise that calls on us to love our neighbor as we love ourselves, but too often love of self comes before love of neighbor.

Propaganda is a dirty word when it comes to the political system, but propaganda can have a potent effect on our voting habits. Indeed, we have a propensity for being swayed by misinformation, which is why campaigns throw mud. Sometimes it's subtle – maybe a commercial that makes use of half-truths or out of context statements. This misinformation can also be very explicit and be spread virally via email or blogs – with the source of the information an unknown. The most obvious example from recent years concerns the continued whispers that that suggests that Barack Obama is foreign born, and thus ineligible to be President, and that he is a Muslim, despite his own strong profession of Christian faith. As long as we allow ourselves to be influenced by such misinformation, it will continue to haunt us. The only way to stop such distortions is for us to do the necessary fact-checking. That, however, takes both time and education.

Talk of spreading democracy to the far corners of the globe seems like a good idea, but it's important to remember that democracy has its dark side. And remember too that even with two-plus centuries of practice, Americans haven't perfected the system. There may not be a better system of governance, but because democracy relies on people, and people according to my theology aren't perfect, this system will never be perfect. The Founders of our nation understood this well, which is why they instituted checks and balances. Besides these checks and balances, we can find hope in grace. We have a chance to grow in our practice of democracy if we learn to extend to one another the grace that has been given to us.

DEMOCRACY CAN BE MESSY!

Americans tend to take democracy for granted, which may be why the percentage of registered voters actually voting is often quite small. But for many people in the world the opportunity to vote freely in relatively fair elections is more dream than reality. Because I value the freedoms that I have as a citizen, I do seek to cast my vote, even if I know that the "other side" may ultimately prevail. Perhaps because we take democracy for granted, we forget that democracy is a rather unpredictable form of governance. Until the votes are cast you don't know who will prevail, and in the end you might not like what you see. Still, we who have this freedom prefer its unpredictability to the alternative.

What I find interesting is the way in which many Americans, who treasure their freedom to choose their own leaders, are less than eager to allow others the same opportunity. When Hamas emerged victorious in Palestinian parliamentary elections some years ago, the American government was dismayed at the results and declared the results unacceptable. When Egypt threw off its American-supported dictator during the recent Arab Spring many in America expressed fears that this would lead to Islamist control of the Egyptian state – as was true in Iran in the 1970s. Whether the Muslim Brotherhood or some other Islamist party will gain control of the Egyptian government remains to be seen, but the point is clear – one may value democracy for one's self and deem it unacceptable for another person. Going back to that Hamas victory, it shouldn't have surprised us that Hamas emerged victorious over a Fatah movement that had not delivered order, peace, or prosperity for the Palestinians. As a result, many Palestinians decided to give the opposition a chance to bring these desired results.

The Middle East is a volatile place, with democracy still in its infancy. Few of America's allies in the region are true democracies, although there is hope that the "Arab Spring" of 2011 will lead to greater openness and a chance at democracy. The fact is, many of our "allies" stayed in power and gained American support because they claimed that they were the last bastion against a radical Islamist takeover. But, if we truly value democracy, shouldn't we be willing to accept the possibility that we won't like the results? After all, we don't always like the results at home either. This is part of what makes democracy what it is – the freedom to make either wise or unwise choices.

Going back to those Palestinian elections – because Palestinian society (as is true in places like Syria as well) has strong secular inclinations, it's not likely that Hamas won in such overwhelming fashion because of its theocratic agenda. In addition, despite a deep seated anger toward Israel among many Palestinians, Hamas seems to have won in such overwhelming fashion in those elections because the reigning party was corrupt, inefficient, and ineffective. Hamas had demonstrated that on at least a limited scale it could provide social services to the Palestinian people and presented themselves as free of corruption. In the long run Hamas has failed to deliver, but that's really not the point.

Political forces such as Hamas face two challenges: dealing with the outside world and governing in such a way that it can provide for the basic needs of the people (order, jobs, homes, water, and food). If they truly embrace the principles of democracy, and succeed in the efforts, they will stay in office. If not, then it would seem the people would make other choices.

Now, I do have worries about the prospects for true democracy when extremists of any sort gain power – whether it's Islamic, Christian, Jewish, Buddhist, Hindu, or secularist. Extremism can be a vice, and often is. The problem with extremists is that they find it difficult to live in peace with those whose views differ from their own. They fail to understand that one can be a "religious exclusivist" and still be a "political pluralist." In the case of groups that have extremist tendencies how will they deal with religious and ethnic minorities? For instance, in the Palestinian territories, the small Christian presence has gotten smaller. The same is true of Iraq. There are fears for the Coptic minority in Egypt and the Christian minority in Syria. There is the question of Israel – can a truly just peace be established where all parties can live together. Fatah recognized Israel, perhaps Hamas will as well. But we have not yet reached that day, so my prayer continues to be that all parties will consider carefully the choices they make.

These are truly unsettled times. There are a whole host of reasons why things could get worse before they get better. Many of those reasons have religious undertones. Democracy is risky in any context, but this is especially true in this corner of the world. Therefore, the future remains uncertain and even dangerous. Yet, there is also room for optimism. If democracy could take hold in Europe and America, it can take firm root elsewhere.

As for me, I will continue to pray and I will continue to dream the impossible dream that one day peace will come to this land called holy. But dreaming is not enough. We must take concrete steps down the pathway of peace. This path can be rocky and dangerous, but there is no other road. As I dream, I will remember Jesus' admonition to love our enemies. I will also remember Paul's admonition to temper my freedoms with love of neighbor. May the love that bridges every chasm prevail!

RED, BLUE, PURPLE: REDEEMING THE "L WORD"

Once upon a time it was a good thing to be liberal, but today it seems that to be a liberal is to be godless and unpatriotic. The word has become so disrespected that many liberals run from the label and call themselves by other names. This is the age of Limbaugh, Hannity, and Coulter.

Not long ago conservative Republicans controlled all three branches of the American government, and conservative church leaders had the President's ear. The once powerful Mainline Protestant churches sat on the sidelines looking back wistfully at what had once been theirs. While the 2008 elections seemed to portend a turning of the tides, it's much too early to tell which way the wind is actually blowing (as the 2010 elections reminded us).

The rise of conservatism is explained by an appeal to ideas. It was said that liberals, unlike conservatives, seemed to lack ideas or a willingness to stand up for what they believe. Of course this isn't really true, but the political and religious right have done a good job at portraying themselves as the true protectors of American political, cultural, and religious values.

It may only be a matter of semantics, because it's quite possible that "liberals" are really "conservatives" and "conservatives" are "liberals." Turning to my trusty *Merriam-Webster OnLine* dictionary I discovered that to be "liberal" is to be free, generous, and broadminded (it can also mean licentious or loose). Freedom, generosity, and broadmindedness would seem to be good American values. That is, to be a liberal people, means that Americans aren't "bound by authoritarianism, orthodoxy, or traditional forms." As for the dictionary definition of the word conservative – I'll deal with that label later.

If you read the definitions of liberal and conservative closely you discover that there is value in both frames of mind. There are traditions, structures, and values worth conserving and preserving, but not everything is worthy of preservation. Surely slavery, Jim Crow, anti-Catholicism, anti-Semitism, the denial of women's suffrage – just to name a few – aren't values and structures worthy of America. At the same time openness and generosity, and freedom of thought and speech are virtues that should be lifted up and preserved; and by definition these are liberal values.

America was born on the premise that the people have the right and the responsibility to question authority and orthodoxy. This requires a broad education and critical thinking. My fear is that we're being tempted, out of fear and maybe ignorance, to jettison these values.

In truth, conservatives and liberals need each other. They provide checks and balances that keep us centered. This is as true in religion as in politics. It's ironic that Mainline Protestantism is often accused of being traditional in its structures and worship, while many conservative Evangelical churches are on the cutting edge of technology and culture.

Being a bit purple myself, I wish to redeem the "L Word." Many religious "liberals" now call themselves "progressives," but there's nothing wrong with being "liberal," especially if by definition this means that one is free, generous, and broad-minded. When it comes to faith, and I'm a pastor after all, there is value in considering the liberal ideal. Although I love the traditions of the church, including its liturgy and music, there's also much value to be found in open conversation, critical study, and the application of reason to faith. Openness to the leadership of women is also a liberal value, as is the commitment to learn from secular thought and from people of other faith traditions. I love the Bible and seek to live out its teachings, but I'm not content to simply believe because "the Bible tells me so." If I'm to profit from its teachings, I must read it responsibly and intelligently.

When it comes to living in a free society, critical thinking and the willingness to grow, even evolve as a human being, is essential. Tradition is important, because it provides us with a sense of rootedness, but tradition can't be left unquestioned. If we wish to continue moving forward as a nation and not become stagnant, then we must hold strongly to the values of freedom (religious and political), generosity, and broadmindedness. And, if this is what it means to be liberal, then I wear the label proudly.

CONSIDERING CONSERVATIVE VALUES

My politics and even my religious perspectives tend to be left of center. By now, if you started reading from the beginning, that confession shouldn't come as any surprise. In a previous essay I tried to reclaim, even redeem, the "liberal" label. Having made that point, I want to say that I also value the true conservative voice. I use the words "true conservative" because what passes for conservativism today is actually quite activist, which runs against the grain of the conservative ideal.

Now, I welcome the conservative voice as a necessary caution to the liberal's advocacy of progressive ideas and actions. This is, of course, the American way, for this nation has never been a one party state. Multiple voices can make for disharmony and confusion, but the alternative is quite unappetizing. If only one voice is heard then freedom of expression has been effectively eliminated.

Our government's system of checks and balances helps prevent one branch of government from dominating the other two, and it keeps us tied to the rule of law. Now, from time to time one party or another will gain ascendancy, but the people have the power to adjust the balance, and often they do just that.

If a liberal is, by definition, open minded, tolerant, and change oriented, the conservative, so the dictionary says, is one who is "averse to change." Conservatism ties itself to the values and institutions of the past, which means the idea of a radical conservative is kind of an oxymoron. I don't know about you, but I find a bit of irony in the label "conservative revolution." That's because a true conservative is cautious and committed to tradition, so to pursue a revolutionary agenda and then try to remake the American way of life, which some modern expressions of conservatism appear to be doing, is anything but conservative.

True conservatism is, however, a check on an overly optimistic and radical liberalism. The conservative voice should caution us against grandiose schemes and ground us in reality. It should call us to be fiscally sound so that the institutions of today may prosper (the Medicare/Social Security debate?). True conservatism remembers and treasures the traditions of nation and religion.

As one church historian said "Tradition is the living faith of the dead, while traditionalism is the dead faith of the living." There is much value to be found in our shared traditions, just as long as they don't become rigid and unreformable. The value of tradition is that it serves as an anchor, without which we tend to lose sight of our purpose and values – such as freedom of speech, freedom of the press, and freedom of religion.

The phrase "throwing the baby out with the bath water" is apropos here. While some things need changing (even radical change), not everything needs changing. Some things are best left alone, like a pristine forest or the habitat of an endangered species. Old buildings may be less efficient, but they give character to a community. Remember that the word conservation derives from the same root as conservative!

What is true of the environment and local architecture is also true in religion and politics. In many ways the American political system has worked quite well for a very long time – two hundred and thirty years and counting. It has needed tweaking and even significant reform, but the basic structures have held up quite well.

Regarding religion, I must confess that my faith is rooted in a book that in its most recent parts is more than nineteen centuries old. I recognize that not everything contained within its pages applies today or even makes sense today, but when responsibly interpreted, it remains the anchor of my faith and millions of others as well. Although I enjoy contemporary forms of worship and new musical expressions, I also love the old hymns and symbols of my faith. In my tradition we practice weekly communion as a way of remembering an event that occurred centuries ago. It's not very modern, but it's still an anchor to my faith.

In many ways I am a liberal, but I appreciate the cautioning voice of the true conservative. This voice allows us to reform our structures and traditions, while keeping us anchored. Change is good – like the growing numbers of women clergy or the prospect that most Americans seem ready to elect a woman or an African American President – but change is most beneficial when it's tempered by a wisdom that's informed by tradition.

THE DARK SIDE OF CERTAINTY

There's something to be said for clarity. When the times require decisiveness, it's good to know what you believe and why. In such life and death moments, time is usually of the essence and you can't second-guess yourself. Needing to act quickly, you have to put off the analysis. It would be great to pause a moment to consider all the ramifications, but you don't have time. Some of your decisions may come back to haunt you, but that's life. After all, you're only human.

Clarity is one thing, absolute certainty is another. If you think you know the truth, and you have no doubts at all, then you're experiencing absolute certainty. Unfortunately, such certainty can keep you from listening to other voices, including voices of experience and wisdom. When you think you (or your group) have all the truth, it's easier to let this certainty lead to untempered zeal and even violent fanaticism.

In a book written by Robert Jewett and John Shelton Lawrence, *Captain America and the Crusade against Evil*, this provocative statement appears: "Common to every contemporary movement that promises salvation through the destruction of others is the doubtful warrant of intense certainty." This book, written post-9/11, serves as a warning to any who would embrace absolute or intense certainty. When you believe with intense certainty, you may become not only passionate but reckless. You may come to believe that the end justifies any means. If, for instance, you can save some lives, then certainly a little torture is justifiable. Or, is it?

We live on an increasingly diverse and interconnected planet. There are few unlinked corners of the earth. To be sure, there are remote outposts in the world, but they become fewer by the day. This increased interaction brings us into contact with ideas, practices, and beliefs that may be markedly different from our own. They raise questions, such as: How do you know your way of doing things is the right way? Is there scientific validation for your culture and values, or do you take it all by faith? Sometimes as we intermingle we may discover that the ways of the other are preferable, and so we choose to adopt this other mode of life. This process is called conversion.

Our interactions can be compromised, however, by stereotype and ignorance of the whole story. Of course, life is easier and more certain when we can live in isolation, whether it's chosen or not, but in the end it's unfruitful and it can be dangerous.

As I look out at the world and see the confusion and conflict, it appears that the world is experiencing growing pains. We're maturing, but in many ways the world has only reached adolescence. Children tend to see things very concretely. There aren't any abstractions, just black and white, which is why Rousseau said it's pointless to try to reason with a child. But with experience and education, we can see the world in broader colors and categories. Adolescence is a period of conflicting emotions and experiences. They're caught between the concrete world of childhood and the abstractions of adulthood.

In the concrete world of the child, there's no room for interpretation, but as we mature we begin to see that things aren't always the way they appear. You have to reason things out and interpret things. Such reasoning makes certainty less viable. There may be objective truth, but it's unlikely that you're an objective observer. Your interpretations are influenced by traditions, society and culture, as well as your own experiences. Ultimately you make choices in faith, hoping that you have all the information you need to choose wisely. Still, in the end it's a matter of faith. The information may come through trial and error or from listening to others; but whatever the source, life has become less black and white.

Jewett and Lawrence caution against embracing intense zeal, but they encourage a modest zeal, or what they call "pilgrim zeal." Such zeal allows for an acknowledgement of the limits to our understanding. It reminds us we're on a journey that hasn't ended. But, such zeal keeps us from falling into indifference and apathy. It's not enough to simply be nice. A better tomorrow demands more of us than that.

LIVING FAITHFULLY WITH AMBIGUITY

Books occasionally appear on the market offering irrefutable proof of Christianity's truth claims. But such claims are not without challenge. Two centuries ago Scottish philosopher David Hume raised the evidentiary bar exceedingly high. Hume insisted that truth was what our senses perceived and confirmed. While many remained steadfast in their beliefs, others were attracted by Hume's skepticism, including some of America's founding fathers. Jefferson and Franklin were Deists who saw value in religion, but sought out a simplified and general creed. Jefferson's famous Bible excised the miraculous from the gospels, leaving behind only Jesus' ethical teachings.

Hume's insistence that we trust only our own experience, places a great burden on the historian and the theologian. If something isn't part of our own experience, then we should skeptical of the reports of others. Now, Hume's call to skepticism has some merit. When I receive an e-mail telling me that I've won the Nigerian lottery I have a right to be skeptical.

But, how far should we go with our skepticism? The scientific method is built on a naturalistic foundation that doubts every answer, pursuing every lead until the truth is known. This allows it to challenge dangerous superstitions and solve seemingly unsolvable problems. Its refusal to stop its inquiry with an appeal to divine will has led to cures for diseases and enabled us to travel to the moon. Therefore, science poses significant challenges to treasured belief systems, including my own.

The challenge, for the believer, is to balance rationality and spirituality. Not being a fan of anti-intellectual religion, I affirm the rationality of God, but I don't believe that theological truth can be known in the same way as scientific truth. In fact, theology and science may talk about the same problem in very different ways, which makes "black and white" answers difficult to come by. This also means that truth isn't always compatible with either/or choices.

Genesis 1 can be true without being historically or scientifically verifiable. And, if you read the four gospels you'll discover four different accounts of Jesus' life. You can try to harmonize them, but in the end loose ends will remain. This doesn't make these accounts untrue or useless, but you won't necessarily find historical precision.

I read the Bible with my mind and with my heart. Faith ultimately has something to do with matters of things hoped for and unseen (Hebrews 11). Therefore, when it comes to proof for God's existence, I don't take my clues from the design of nature – which often gives conflicting reports. Instead, I look to the spiritual longings of humanity. This isn't fool proof, but I find it compelling.

Religion can be a catalyst for good or ill. In many ways it's what we make of it. As a Christian I find my faith tradition compelling, truthful, and satisfying. My experiences with people of other religions have taught me that they too live meaningful lives and seem to have discernable relationships with God. It's interesting too that something akin to the golden rule is present in almost every religion. Could this not be evidence of God's presence in the world?

I'm a person of faith, but I've become comfortable with questions, doubt, and ambiguity. I believe in truth, but I don't believe that I have the corner on that truth. Ultimately the final arbiter of truth is in the hands of someone greater than me, which means I'm not competent to judge my neighbor.

When it comes to the question of objective truth, I find myself wanting to be cautious. Truth may be objective, but that doesn't mean that I have an objective grasp of truth. When it comes to religion and faith in God, there must be room for doubt. We must be comfortable with metaphor and analogy. Jesus told parables, which are stories that tell truth, but the stories themselves are fiction. I have doubts and questions, but I remain a person of deep and abiding faith. God is not, for me, a fantasy, but I remain cautious in my assertions of truth. This isn't a vice, in fact, in an age of religiously inspired intolerance and even violence, a bit of caution might be warranted.

THE DANGERS OF TRIUMPHALISM

Palm Sunday, in the Christian tradition, celebrates Jesus' "triumphal entry" into Jerusalem. The Gospels picture a crowd hailing Jesus as Israel's deliverer from Roman occupation, but as the story continues, we discover that the crowd has misinterpreted the signs. Jesus, it seems, has a different mission, one that calls into question the whole premise of a "triumphal entry."

Instead, Jesus dies on an imperial Roman cross. Christians, including me, are tempted to skip over the dark clouds of Good Friday to the triumph of Easter, for we would prefer good news to bad, victory to defeat, winners over losers. Indeed, in some sectors of the Christian community, there is a growing preference for the "muscular Jesus" to the "gentle shepherd Jesus."

As a nation we like to celebrate the winners, the heroes, the strong and the powerful. We want leaders who will lead us to victory, whether the game is basketball, war, or the economy. And so, we're tempted by "triumphalism," which, as theologian Douglas John Hall writes, is that tendency afflicting all world views, whether religious or secular, to see themselves "as full and complete accounts of reality, leaving little if any room for debate or difference of opinion and expecting of their adherents unflinching belief and loyalty." (Hall, 17). You are, as they say, either with us or against us, and any hesitation will be taken as a sign that you're really not with us.

When religious people enter the public arena they often come in under a triumphalist guise, what historian Mark Toulouse calls "priestly faith." This "priestly faith" is a distorted form of religion that merges the religious with the national agenda to such a degree that they become indistinguishable. Thus, nation becomes confused with church (or synagogue, mosque, temple, etc.). It's the type of faith that celebrates America as a "Christian nation," and takes public symbols and fills them with religious, indeed, with Christian meanings.

Consider for a moment an issue that has gotten people riled up in recent years: the phrase "under God" in the Pledge of

Allegiance. This phrase wasn't in the original pledge, which dates back to the late 19th century. It was added in the mid-1950s during the early days of the Cold War, as a response to a perceived threat from the "Godless Communists" of the Soviet Union (my, doesn't that sound dated?). Congress also changed the national motto from "*E Pluribus Unum*" (from the many, one) to "In God We Trust." In so doing, the American government declared that we are the godly ones.

Advocates and practitioners of this "priestly faith" first infuse public symbols with religious meaning and then declare that these meanings "represent the only true way of being both Christian and American" (Toulouse, 82). Popular during the 'dark days" of the 1950s, when school children practiced "ducking and covering," this "priestly faith" has made a rebound in recent years. Now, however, the "enemy" isn't the "Godless Communist," but is instead the "Islamofascist Terrorists." With this change of enemies, the generic Judeo-Christian God of the 1950s requires further definition. Now the battle isn't between the godless and the godly, but between adherents of what many in America believe are two different Gods – the Christian versus the Muslim. With Miroslav Volf, I would insist that Christians and Muslims, as well as Jews, worship the same God (Volf, *Allah*).

Too often religious faith is merged into a nationalism that distorts our faith traditions, so that they become tools of national interests. If we're to find any semblance of peace in an ethnically and religiously diverse nation and world, then we must find a different way of living faithfully in the public square. Triumphalism inhibits our ability to listen to the voice of the other, because to such a mind, the other has no value to us. If one stands outside the circle, they must be assimilated, shunned, or if necessary destroyed.

Palm Sunday, when seen from the vantage point of Good Friday, is ultimately a dead end. And, if we believe we must win at all costs – whether the conflict involves religions, rival gangs, or nation states – we will destroy ourselves. The "triumphalist" way has been judged by God and has been found wanting. This means that we must find a different way, one that is humble and ready to listen to the other.

AMERICA'S MANIFEST DESTINY?

Manifest Destiny is deeply rooted in the American psyche. We have tended to see ourselves destined by Providence to spread our influence and values across the world. It fueled the westward movement of the 19th century and it gave impetus to the missionary movement of the late 19th and early 20th centuries – when Jesus and American values were carried together to all parts of the world. It also fueled Christian support for wars with Mexico and Spain.

To give but one example – Lyman Abbott, a Congregationalist minister and Social Gospeler, gave voice to an American imperialism in his reflections on the Spanish-American War:

> "We fought the American Revolution to free ourselves, the Civil War to free a people whom we had helped to enslave, the Spanish-American War to free a people to whom we owed no other duty than that of a big nation to an oppressed nation" (Abbott, 438).

He expressed a common vision that it was proper for the United States to extend its imperial reach into the Caribbean and on to the Philippines. It was our destiny!

From the earliest days, Americans have defined our national identity in terms of exceptionalism and innocence. We tend to see ourselves as somehow different from other nations, for we're seemingly untainted by their "sins." In our self-understanding, we see ourselves carrying out our duties with selflessness and without imperial designs. This perception of ourselves makes it difficult for Americans to understand why other peoples harbor ill-will towards us. Why, we wonder, do they resist our gifts of freedom?

Returning to Lyman Abbott's glowing comments about American designs in the Spanish-American War, the famed preacher ignored the fact that the Philippine people didn't welcome our occupation and fought a three-year war against American occupational forces (1899 to 1902). Of course, the history of

European-American engagement with Native Americans is another painful reminder of the legacy of Manifest Destiny. It seems that the gift of freedom often comes at the cost of submission to another imperial power.

As the reigning Super Power in the world, we have become in a sense the New Rome, and like this earlier empire we seek to extend our influence around the world because of our interests in those parts of the world. Although Rome offered a *Pax Romana* or Roman Peace, it came at a price. Living, then and now, under the influence of the empire offers innumerable benefits and blessings, but there are tradeoffs. The empire expects a certain amount of obeisance.

Then, as now, the empire rooted its claims in an imperial theology, a religious ideology that helped define the empire's identity and purpose. Claims that America is a Christian nation are often combined with support for and even rationales for the extension of American power around the world. In making the claim, advocates of this ideology merge a religious identity with a national identity and insist that God has a special purpose for the nation.

As a follower of Jesus, I'm reminded that he died on an imperial cross because he proclaimed a different kind of kingdom – the Kingdom of God. The foundation of this kingdom is radically different from that of any empire – for it is rooted not in violence but nonviolence. Caesar understood that to give allegiance to God is to take it away from him, and Caesar demanded total allegiance.

Since the time of Constantine, Christians have subsumed the message of the Kingdom of God under that of the Empire and have made Jesus the Empire's patron. Indeed, whenever we who are Christians merge our Christian identity with our American identity by proclaiming this to be a Christian nation, we make Jesus the foundation of empire.

For America or any nation to consider itself Christian, it must answer "Kingdom of God" kinds of questions, such as how the nonviolent teachings of Jesus should define our foreign policy. We would have to consider how his teachings influence policies toward the poor, the indigent, the young and the elderly. When we hear presidents and presidential candidates speak of their faith, we should then ask them about the relationship between that faith and their actions and decisions. Ultimately the question has to do with our loyalties – to whom shall we bow? Are we citizens of the Empire, or of the Kingdom?

AMERICA AND ITS ICONIC BIBLE

A controversy concerning the use of the Qur'an in Congressional oath-taking ceremonies raised the question of the Bible's place in American life. Radio host Dennis Prager laid down the gauntlet in a much publicized column when he said:

> Insofar as a member of Congress taking an oath to serve America and uphold its values is concerned, America is interested in only one book, the Bible. If you are incapable of taking an oath on that book, don't serve in Congress.

If the Bible is America's Holy Book, what exactly does that mean? It's true that the Bible is regularly used in a variety of public ceremonies, from swearing in of witnesses to oath-taking by public officials. It's believed that using the Bible in such a way guarantees truthfulness, although there's little evidence that such use prevents either corruption or perjury.

When we talk about the Bible as America's Holy Book, we're not talking about its content; we're talking about its symbolic status. Indeed, that's Prager's point. Therefore, since the Bible is essentially an object of veneration, we dutifully trot it out whenever we deem it appropriate. If necessary we'll read it selectively in support of our pet projects. Take for instance the Ten Commandments: many venerate them, but spend little time examining their meaning.

The Bible's iconic value is connected to America's mythical "Judeo-Christian" heritage, something that's apparently now under siege by pluralists and immigrants alike. Reference is often made to the nation's golden age when that heritage is assumed to have reigned supreme. However, a close reading of America's history suggests that the story is much more complicated than that. Besides, there are dark shadows that lay across our nation's religious heritage, from slavery to segregation. Nonetheless the Bible is often regarded as synonymous with American life. The tradition of using the Bible to take the Presidential Oath of Office dates back to George Washington, who used his Masonic Bible in that ceremony.

We've had presidentially-decreed "Years of the Bible," while speech writers pepper political speeches with biblical allusions, often taken out of context. To give but one example: President Bush, in a speech following 9-11, said "the light shines in the darkness. And the darkness will not overcome it." He was referring to America, but the passage (John 1:5) refers not to our nation but to Jesus' entrance into the world. The iconic stature of the Bible, Mark Toulouse writes, "subordinates biblical values to whatever American political thought might need at the moment" (Toulouse, 61).

Upwards of 93% of us own a Bible, and somewhere around 82% believe it to be divinely inspired. No wonder so many people embrace Creationist views. Unfortunately, there's also significant evidence that Americans know very little about the Bible's content. To give an example, in a Gallup poll only 49% of Americans could name the first book of the Bible (Genesis) and only 34% of us knew who delivered the Sermon on the Mount (it's Jesus by the way).

For the Christian, however, the Bible should be more than simply a national icon that we venerate but ignore in our daily life. Instead, it should inform our faith and our practice as Christians. The same could be said for religious Jews as well. It should challenge us to walk with God and walk humbly and peaceably with our neighbor (Micah 6:8). And so we who wish to take the Bible seriously need to heed this reminder by Mark Toulouse:

> When the nation uses the Bible in iconic fashion, the nation honors the book as a symbol instead of taking the book seriously for its content. In this context, politicians, and even ministers and Christian social activists, can easily slip into the political misuse of the Bible's content to suit their own purposes (*Ibid*, 63).

God hasn't made special covenant with the United States of America. Whatever covenants God has made transcend national boundaries.

As one who finds the words of the Bible to be enriching and

challenging, I believe its words must be interpreted carefully and very seriously. To do otherwise, especially if the Bible is read or used in a politicized way, could be dangerous. Therefore, I'll take my Bible seriously but not as a national icon.

Ruling by Divine Mandate?

In a conversation with a friend I was stunned by his insistence that God chooses our presidents for us. Apparently God is guiding the nation's voters – or at least the Electoral College. My friend found the constant criticisms of the President Bush, including my own, troubling and inappropriate – for we're to honor our leaders and support them. Now, things might have changed since that conversation, as the person holding that office has changed. His beliefs, which I don't think are unique, have a long history – they're rooted in a tradition of "divine right monarchy." This ideology of earlier years held that because God is sovereign and God chooses the ruler, from family to nation, we who are ruled should not resist that person's judgments. We should, instead, trust in the ruler's judgment – for surely they know more than do we about the affairs of state.

The idea that our leaders lead with a divine mandate often seeks to draw from biblical precedents, such as David's reticence to touch Saul because he was God's anointed (1 Samuel 26:9). Then there's this verse from Paul's letter to the Romans:

> "Let every person be subject to the governing authorities; for there is no authority except from God, and those authorities that exist have been instituted by God" (Romans 13:1 NRSV).

That seems rather direct and to the point, but what we tend to forget when we read and try to apply a passage such as this is that it has its own context. We forget that the governing authorities mentioned here are Imperial Rome and its proxies. Perhaps Paul was cautioning prospective rebels to reconsider. What this passage doesn't have in mind is American-style democracy, where at least in principle the people are the foundation of government.

That was my answer to my friend's statement – we the people choose the president of the United States – sometimes we make good choices and at other times not so good choices, as history has demonstrated. Because the people make the choice, the

President – this President and every President – is therefore accountable to the people of this country. This point needs to be made at a time when the religious rhetoric in the public sphere is becoming increasingly sharp.

As we wrestle with texts like Romans 13 that encourage us to obey our leaders, we need to remember that our nation was founded in the midst of a revolution that threw off the designated governing authority – King George III. We should also remember that if we take Romans 13 very literally and apply it indiscriminately, then we must apply it not just to our leaders who are democratically elected, but to all leaders – including Hitler, Stalin, and yes even Saddam Hussein.

If a leader believes himself or herself to be divinely chosen, or if that person's supporters speak in terms of divine mandate, that ideology will certainly steel them up when making difficult choices. But such a sensibility can prove to be dangerous, for to believe that one carries a divine mandate creates blind spots and insulates them from listening to advice that runs counter to their agenda. Indeed, leaders could delude themselves into thinking it appropriate to "go it alone" despite the opposition or misgivings of allies. And when combined with a vision of "American Exceptionalism," such a sense of divine calling could lead to an arrogant expansion of American imperialism around the world.

With a growing number of candidates for office on both sides of the partisan divide expressing themselves in religious terms; it's important that we remind them that as elected leaders they have a responsibility to the people. If they're people of faith, then their faith traditions can and should help guide their decision making – hopefully making them more compassionate, more gracious, and more committed to justice and peace – but ultimately they must remember that the people have chosen them to lead, and it's to the people that they're accountable.

If I understand Paul in his context, I can hear him remind us that God desires order not chaos. But if there is any divine mandate to be considered it is our calling as people to exercise good judgment in choosing our leaders, and then having chosen them we should pray for them but also show due diligence by holding them accountable to the highest standards.

EXTREMISM: A 21ST CENTURY IDEOLOGY?

If totalitarianism was the great problem of the twentieth century, then extremism is, so far, the great problem of the twenty-first.

This is our future, says former *Newsweek* editor Jon Meacham. News reports would seem to support his analysis. Jihads, Crusades, and Culture Wars dominate daily conversation, while ideology polarizes us. You're either for or against us, and either red or blue, with no room for purple.

While Hitler, Mussolini, Mao, and Stalin dominated the last century, religious and cultural extremism now grab the headlines. Osama bin Laden was more driven by religious fanaticism than desire for power, with his followers willing to sacrifice their lives for the cause through suicide bombings. Though it's easy to point the finger at an Osama Bin Laden, he's not alone. I might be comparing apples and oranges, but listen for a moment to Pat Robertson. Zealotry is very much part of his ideology, as seen in the encouragement he gave (despite a later apology) for the assassination of a foreign head of state and his prayers for "miraculous" openings on the Supreme Court. Though Robertson's followers haven't strapped on bomb-laden vests, there is a violent tendency to his rhetoric. And if we think that our own religious tradition is incapable of violence, then a close reading of Mark Juergensmeyer's *Terror in the Mind of God* is urgently needed. He demonstrates that the impulse to extremist violence is present in every religious tradition and not just Islam.

But what is extremism? Barry Goldwater once said "that extremism in the defense of liberty is no vice. And . . . moderation in the pursuit of justice is no virtue." Now, if moderation means acquiescence to injustice, then surely extremism might be the better course of action. Ironically, years later the late Senator from Arizona decried the extremism he believed had overtaken his party: "When you say 'radical right' today, I think of these moneymaking ventures by fellows like Pat Robertson and others who are trying to take the Republican Party away from the Republican Party and make a religious organization out of it. If that ever happens, kiss politics goodbye" (*Washington Post,* July 28, 1994).

In his day Martin Luther King, Jr. was considered by many to be an extremist. So extreme was he that the FBI kept him under constant surveillance. Writing from his Birmingham jail cell, King defended his extremism: "The question is not whether we will be extremist but what kind of extremist will we be. Will we be extremists for hate or will we be extremists for love? Will we be extremists for the preservation of injustice—or will we be extremists for the cause of justice?"

The definition of extremism would appear to be a matter of interpretation, with the times and context influencing our definitions; remember that to most people in England George Washington was an extremist. Strong opposition to injustice and oppression can be seen by some as fanaticism, and it's easy to paint advocates of change with the charge of extremism, but true extremism emerges from a narrow and polarizing ideology that can easily become coercive and even violent. Whereas the last century's ideologies were often rooted in radical secularism, this century's radicals are too often motivated by religion.

We all know about Muslim extremists who blow themselves up pursuit of their cause, but there have also been extremist Christians who show vulgar intolerance and even violence in pursuit of their causes. Anti-abortionist Paul Hill felt driven to kill a physician while Fred Phelps offers up hate-filled messages to gays and lesbians. These may not be run of the mill Christians, but they claim the name and justify their views and actions by turning to the Bible.

There is nothing wrong with being committed to one's faith or one's political principles, but if one's zeal turns into a fanaticism that threatens to tear apart the fabric of human society, then things have gone too far. For, instead of being the glue that holds society together and the voice that challenges injustice; religion becomes a centrifugal force that drives society apart in the name of God. Religion should fight for justice, but it should also build bridges and cement disparate elements of society. The hope for the future requires us to chart a middle course.

READ MY LIPS – TALKING TAXES

Mark Twain wrote: "What is the difference between a taxidermist and a tax collector? The taxidermist takes only your skin." Anti-tax sentiments like Twain's aren't a new phenomenon – Jesus was criticized for hanging out with tax collectors. So unpopular is the levying of taxes that no politician would dare run on a platform of raising taxes. He or she may make all sorts of promises about bringing benefits to the voter, but that politician would be fool-hardy to say how he or she would pay for these benefits.

We live in a credit happy nation, with a consumer debt as large as the federal one. We're a bit like Wimpy – "I'd gladly pay you Tuesday, for a hamburger today." As a result, we go to war, expend billions each week, and cut taxes. Politicians talk about cutting pork, but no one agrees as to what counts as pork. I don't like paying taxes any more than the next person, but if our government is going to provide us services, then we must pay for them.

The basic issue is the level of services we expect government to provide. The Constitution speaks of providing for the nation's defense and the general welfare of the people, but what does this involve? To answer the question, we must get beyond the "small vs. large government" debate by first recognizing that more than half our tax dollars go to fund the military and pay interest on the debt. Then there's Social Security and Medicare, both of which were designed to pay for themselves; however recipients will soon equal the number of payers. Government also provides for education, police and fire, roads and bridges, and more. It's true that some funds do get misused, but how much pork can be eliminated so that tax cuts pay for themselves? If that amount is really minimal, then what services are we willing to give up?

The clause in the Constitution that allows for taxes states:

> "The Congress shall have power to lay and collect Taxes, Duties, Imposts and Excises, to pay the Debts and provide for the common Defence and general

Welfare of the United States; . . . " (Article 1, Section 8, Clause 1).

Even if the definition of general welfare in the 18th century was rather narrow – that is, government didn't provide what charities once provided – must we not recognize that the context has changed. We are a much more diverse and larger community now than then. Even then the problems of providing for the poor and indigent were greater than traditional charities could address, and now the issues are broader and larger than ever. Only the government has access to the resources necessary to tackle the big issues of the day.

Consider Katrina: The congregation I served at the time gave generously, as did many nonprofits, religious groups, and businesses. But the job was much too big for them to handle on their own. They played a role, but more was needed. Social Security was enacted in 1935 to provide a safety net for seniors who had fallen through the cracks. Unemployment benefits assist workers in paying the rent and feeding their families. And the list goes on.

If we believe that the nation's general welfare requires some kind of safety net, then we must face the question of how to pay for it. Payment requires taxation, but not all taxes are equal. Some would argue that everyone should pay the same amount or the same proportion – perhaps as a flat tax or as a sales or value- added tax. That seems fair, at first, but consider that a sales tax hits lower income people harder. The graduated nature of the income tax assumes that the wealthier one is, the more discretionary income one has, and thus is better able to contribute.

Despite our aversion to paying taxes – and I'm no more eager to pay them than the next person – it would seem that they are a necessity. Without them, the government services we receive – including roads and bridges, police and fire protection, hospitals and civil defense, would be impossible. So the next time you hear a politician talk about tax cuts, ask yourself what part of the common defense and the general welfare you're willing to do without.

JUSTICE IN THE LAND

AM I MY BROTHER'S KEEPER?

The credo of partisan politics often is: Do what's best for the party, even if it's not what's best for the nation. And the credo of nationalism is: Do what's best for our nation, even if that's not what's best for the world as a whole. Politicians know that if they take care of their party members, their constituents, and maybe even on occasion their fellow citizens (of their nation) they will be rewarded for their service to the narrow good.

All of this is rooted in an individualistic philosophy, a philosophy that is exemplified in the resurgent popularity of Ayn Rand's call to selfishness. It's a world view that proclaims that we must look out for ourselves, because no one else will. Therefore, I'll do what's best for me, and as for my neighbor – that's their problem.

The opposite of such a philosophy is a commitment to pursue the common good. Commitment to the common good sounds wonderful, but it seems out of place in an increasingly partisan, sectarian, and nationalist era. Rarely do we hear these days that rallying cry of John Kennedy: "And so, my fellow Americans, ask not what your country can do for you; ask what you can do for your country." And thinking even more broadly, Dwight D. Eisenhower could say: "This world of ours ... must avoid becoming a community of dreadful fear and hate, and be, instead, a proud confederation of mutual trust and respect." And then there's this statement by Barbara Jordan, the late Congresswoman from Texas, which reminds us that "a nation is formed by the willingness of each of us to share in the responsibility for upholding the common good."

Cain asked God, "Am I my brother's keeper." God's answer is "yes, you are." I believe that a case can be made for the premise that the world is better off when we pursue the common good. But pursuit of the common good requires that we balance our own personal needs with the needs of others. It means that the majority respect the rights and needs of those who are in the minority. It means recognizing that the acts and decisions of one nation often impact the lives of other nations – global warming for instance transcends boundaries. Therefore, commitment to the common good may require of us at the very least a degree of self-denial and self-sacrifice.

What then are the practical implications of the principle that I'm called by God to be my "brother's keeper"? One might consider the implications of these case studies. For instance, what value do I derive from paying taxes to support a public educational system if I don't have children in the system? Respondents might question why, since their children are grown or because they don't have children, they should pay to educate someone else's child. There are a number of answers to this question, but consider the benefits of having a knowledgeable and productive workforce, reduction in juvenile crime and violence, and maybe even population stabilization. Now not everyone is equally gifted, but if we're committed to the common good, then a child should at least be given a chance at success. Medical care is another area of common concern. The current system does a great job of serving those who can afford good insurance, but what about the millions of people who are uninsured or under-insured? What of their welfare? Furthermore, even if you're not all that concerned about the welfare of someone else; what about the impact on you if disease begins to spread through the broader community? It's impossible to totally wall ourselves off from the health issues of the broader world, for epidemics are no respecters of persons.

Even when we don't receive a direct benefit of our contributions to society, we receive benefits indirectly. That's the blessing of considering the common good. I might not get everything I want, but I'll be better off living in a world where the community as a whole has good health care, strong educational opportunities, public safety, and cultural opportunities. If ever we understood the need for a strong government, it was during Hurricane Katrina. Because the nation's emergency preparedness was left in the hand of an unprepared political appointee, hundreds died or were left stranded during a devastating storm.

Ultimately, we're all in this together. What affects you will ultimately affect me, and the world will be better off when we finally learn this lesson. So, the truth is, I am my brother's and my sister's keeper.

DREAMING OF THE PROMISED LAND
WITH ROSA AND MARTIN

Rosa Parks' small act of defiance changed history. Her death in 2005 was marked by acts of remembrance fit for a national leader or military hero, but Rosa Parks was neither a politician nor a military hero. To the unknowing, Rosa was a black woman too tired to get up so that a white man could have his "rightful" seat on a Montgomery, Alabama bus. Whether intended or not, her "act of defiance" and subsequent arrest, sparked a movement that changed America.

A young Baptist pastor picked up Rosa's cause and organized a bus boycott that set in motion a movement that would knock down segregation's shameful barriers to the American dream. In short order Jim Crow gave way, and buses, schools, lunch counters, and water fountains were integrated. A decade later Congress followed suit and passed the Voting Rights Act, eliminating another legal barrier to equality.

America has not been the same since Rosa Parks refused to give up her seat and a young pastor took up and embodied the cause of equality in America. It is not surprising that the establishment of Martin Luther King's birthday as a national holiday was shrouded in controversy. After all, the Civil Rights Movement had let out of the closet a skeleton that had blighted American life since the nation's birth. History has shown Dr. King to be an imperfect vessel, but his courage and leadership in the face of overwhelming public opposition changed America for the better. Slavery may have ended in 1865, but its legacy of bigotry and discrimination remained enshrined in American law and culture for another century.

Only thirty-nine when an assassin's bullet cut short his life, Dr. King's dream of a society marked by equality and equanimity has lived on. Like Moses, King bore within himself the mantle of leadership. He heard the call of those crying out for relief from bondage. He made it to the mountain top and he looked into the Promised Land, but as with Moses it would not be his destiny to cross the river. But, the dream lived on and the people crossed the river and we as a nation began to create a society where character and not one's color or one's ethnicity or gender would define one's place.

Dr. King dreamt that "one day this nation will rise up and live out the true meaning of its creed: 'we hold these truths to be self-evident: that all men are created equal'." On that day freedom will ring out from every village, hamlet, state and city, and "all of God's children, black men and white men, Jews and Gentiles, Protestants and Catholics, will be able to join hands and sing in the words of the old Negro spiritual, "Free at last! Free at last! Thank God Almighty, we are free at last!" It is imperative that this dream not be forgotten. We have made progress since Rosa Parks chose to keep her seat, but the work is not finished.

Dr. King's dream challenged and helped shape my world view, but I have lived this dream imperfectly. As a white male I am the beneficiary of a privileged status, and I must be reminded of my calling to bear witness to this dream of freedom, dignity, and equality for all. This is especially true at a time when decades of progress are threatened by retrenchment that seeks to undermine affirmative action programs and voting rights laws. Corporate America remains overly white and male, while white males continue to dominate America's governments and courts from the local level to the federal. There has also been an increase in bigotry and discrimination in our society, especially toward Muslims and Latinos. The achievement gap separating white America from non-white America is widening. Things may be better than they were in 1955, but we have yet to achieve Dr. King's dream of a day when character rather than color or economic status determines one's fate. Tomorrow's day of remembrance reminds us that we must not rest until all people, no matter their race, ethnicity, economic status, gender, religion, sexual orientation, or level of education, receive all their rights and responsibilities enshrined in the Declaration of Independence.

Taking a stand for what's right – Nonviolently

The Civil Rights Movement of the 1950s and 1960s, a movement that is identified with the life of Martin Luther King, Jr., helped end Jim Crow laws and rendered segregation in America illegal. Most of all, it affirmed the equality of every person in this country. His opposition to all forms of segregation and his affirmation of human dignity continue to influence American life to this day. Although he died of an assassin's bullet, his example lives on whenever we seek to emulate his life and message.

Taking his cues from Mahatma Gandhi and Jesus of Nazareth, King engaged the "powers that be." Choosing the way of non-violence meant that his was a revolution without guns or even stones. Utilizing marches and sit-ins, he brought a moral force to the debates of the day. He didn't choose to seek change violently, but neither did he passively acquiesce to the societal abuses of the day. Not everyone embraced his methods. Some thought they were too slow, while others thought they went too far and too fast. Yet, Martin Luther King remains a model for us, showing us that non-violence can achieve the aims we pursue.

Because Dr. King looked to Jesus as his guide, it would be important to consider some of Jesus' guiding statements. He said things like: "If anyone strikes you on the right cheek, turn the other also" and "If any one forces you to go one mile, go also the second mile." To some this appears to encourage passivity in the face of injustice, as if Jesus was saying: "Just do as you're told." But is this what Jesus had in mind? Is his call for meekness a call to passivity? I think there's more to this than meets the eye and I think Dr. King understood this quite well.

Recent biblical scholarship offers a different perspective on these sayings. Instead of encouraging passive acceptance of one's lot in life, even if they are oppressive, Jesus offers his audience —most of whom were from the lower classes and often felt the brunt of Roman occupation – a non-violent way of achieving equality. To turn the other cheek or to walk the second mile is to take responsibility for one's own life and destiny. Biblical scholar Walter Wink writes:

He is helping an oppressed people find a way to protest and neutralize an onerous practice despised throughout the empire. He is not giving a nonpolitical message of spiritual world transcendence. He is formulating a worldly spirituality in which the people at the bottom of society or under the thumb of imperial power learn to recover their humanity (Wink, 108).

Dr. King's movement was just that. It was a spiritually empowered movement that helped people reclaim their humanity. In turning the other cheek they helped turn the nation upside down nonviolently, but effectively.

In remembering Dr. King's birthday, let's not think that we've yet achieved his dream of a nation where differences in ethnicity, religion, language, gender, or sexual orientation no longer matter. Our celebration only serves to remind us that much remains to be done. As long as barriers to prevent people from finding their equal place in society and people remain voiceless, there will be work to do.

In many ways we stand at a crossroads in our nation's history. Today we have an African American serving as President and in 2008 a woman made a credible run for the nation's top office. No longer must we wonder whether we're ready for such a thing, though we need to recognize that the feeling isn't unanimous.

We've come a long way in our national attempt to truly live out the premises contained in the Declaration of Independence. This document declares "that all men are created equal, that they are endowed by their Creator with certain unalienable Rights, that among these are Life, Liberty, and the pursuit of Happiness." But, as Dr. King knew, this isn't just about rights; it's also about our responsibility to join together in creating a community that is just and fair, safe and full of hope and opportunity for all people.

REDEEMING THE "NERD" – VALUING EDUCATION

Taped-together black horn-rimmed glasses, high-water pants, and a pocket protector are the Nerd's uniform. Nerd is a metaphor for the smart but goofy student. Exploited by television and film, the stereotype leaves the lasting impression that being smart isn't cool. It is an anti-intellectual metaphor, one that distorts the value of the mind and devalues education. In an age when education is a harbinger of one's future, it would seem appropriate to challenge the metaphor and encourage the life of the mind.

Although the Bible speaks of loving God with mind as well as heart and soul, religion can be and often is anti-intellectual, contributing to the devaluation of education and knowledge. Most religious traditions value wisdom and knowledge, with the sage or wisdom teacher being honored above all others. Though he is often the butt of childish jokes, Confucius has been for centuries the defining figure of Chinese culture, while Solomon is regaled for his wisdom.

The biblical book of Proverbs honors the one who seeks wisdom, "for learning about wisdom and instruction, for understanding words of insight, for gaining instruction in wise dealing, righteousness, justice, and equity; to teach shrewdness to the simple, knowledge and prudence to the young . . ." (Proverbs 1:2-5). In this biblical tradition there is no higher calling than the pursuit of knowledge and wisdom. In an age that honors celebrities, this pursuit of knowledge has lost its glamour, but the future of our society depends in large part on knowledge and wisdom.

A society that doesn't value wisdom will not value the education of its children.

While much is made of the need for accountability and reform in public education, the real issue isn't teacher performance or tenure, it's one of societal values. The misguided and malformed "No Child Left Behind" mandate is symptomatic of easy fix solutions that don't deal with the basic issue – our neglect of the life of the mind. All that NCLB has done is humiliate an underfunded and underappreciated public school system. We can change tenure rules and institute mandatory testing, but unless we as a society truly value the pursuit of wisdom and knowledge reform will fail.

I am married to a former teacher, who is the daughter of a teacher and the sister and sister-in-law of teachers. I am a parent whose child has graduated from public schools. I have been a student myself and I've taught in colleges and graduate schools. So, I believe I have a little experience with the educational system. It's not perfect and there are the occasional bad apples and scores of underperforming schools. Still, most teachers are committed to their vocation and doing the best they can with limited resources and often with limited parental and community support. What could they do if they were provided a bit more money, more parental support, and even more community support?

Ultimately change will come when we realize that education is more than learning to add numbers and read words. It is more than simply a tool to make a living. Education is about exploring the universe in all its complexity. It involves learning to read, write, add and subtract, but it also involves the exploration of music, philosophy, literature, science, and yes religion. The old "liberal arts" education was designed to form a well rounded citizen. That's a still a good idea!

One of my greatest concerns today has to do with the lack of civility in public discourse. It afflicts young and old, conservative and liberal. Maybe if we "redeem the nerd" and elevate the pursuit of wisdom, we will also restore civility to the public square. The issue here is not about levels of education or blue collar versus white collar. It's really a matter of valuing, what I as a Christian would hold to be the divine gifts of wisdom and knowledge that form the basis of civilization. When we value curiosity and questioning of things, then we will be ready to learn from each other.

This pursuit of knowledge and wisdom has value for the religious community as well as the general populace. Though I value religious experience, unfettered and unreasoned experience, can be dangerous. In the summary of the Law, we are commanded to love God with "all your heart, soul, mind, and strength." May we seek this balance and honor God by using our minds to their fullest. By doing this, we will redeem not only the nerd, but society as a whole.

MUGGLES, MUDBLOODS, AND OTHER OBJECTS OF BIGOTRY

No one likes to think of themselves as bigots, but unfortunately bigotry remains a present challenge to our society. Discussions of immigration policy, national security, even marriage often contain veiled and not so veiled statements about "them." "Them" is code for those we deem undesirable; those who would steal our jobs, pollute our culture, waste our tax payer dollars, or undermine our morality. Yes, bigotry remains a problem in our day.

I happen to be a big Harry Potter fan, and as I read these books over the years I couldn't help but hear the book's author speaking to this very issue that plagues our world today. Supposedly this is a series of children's books, but they are much more, for many adults have found not just hours of enjoyment, but deep meaning in this increasingly mature series of books. The books offer insight into such virtues as friendship, loyalty, being true to one's self, and the importance of standing up for those who cannot stand up for themselves.

J.K. Rowling seems to have understood the old adage that truth must be caught rather than taught, and therefore it's quite possible to read these books, especially the final volume, as a protest against the rising tide of bigotry in our world today. In the case of Harry Potter's world, the bigotry comes from the wizarding world's "Purebloods," and it's directed against "Muggles" (non-wizards) and "Muggle-borns" or "Mudbloods," as radical "Purebloods" love to call them. "Mud-bloods" are wizards like Hermione Granger and Harry's mother, Lily, who are without any apparent "wizarding" ancestry. Their "powers" are therefore seen as somehow illegitimate – even stolen.

This bigotry among wizards might be traced to the fact that they must live in the shadows, something many resent. But it's also born of a sense of superiority, and as we all know – "might makes right." Their desire to keep things pure leads some radicalized "Purebloods" to engage in a policy of oppression and even murder. And those "purebloods" who sympathize with these "lower beings" are seen as traitors – "blood-traitors" – who must be marginalized for their love of "Muggles" and "Mudbloods." But even our heroes must learn something about bigotry, and it's the "Muggle-born" Hermione Granger who is their teacher. She helps her friends see other non-human beings –like the house-elves who are essentially slaves – as having dignity and honor in their own right.

If any of this sounds familiar, it should, for this morality-play sheds light on our own histories and experiences. A fanatical concern for racial purity stood at the heart of the Nazi's Aryan ideology, but they're not alone in history. Consider our own American legacy of slavery, Jim Crow, and the Trail of Tears, just to give a few examples.

Yes this isn't just a series of fantasy stories meant for children (indeed this is a series of books that has matured with the original readers of the series). It is a word of wisdom that we can learn from as we deal with a world that's becoming increasingly diverse and yet increasingly intolerant. Indeed, it can be said that bigotry is on the rise everywhere in the world today. Here in America the traditional recipients of bigotry – African Americans, Roman Catholics, Asians, and Jews – have been joined by Latinos, Gays, Muslims, and immigrants of all stripes, but especially those who hail from Mexico and Central America.

It seems that we regularly read and hear laments about the threats to American security and culture from those who are different. Despite the fact – with the possible exception of Native Americans – that there is no such thing as a truly "blue-blooded American" – we all stem from immigrant stock – some believe themselves to be more American than others. But such bigotry is never right and is often a pretext to discrimination and to violence. It is, in fact, repugnant to what's right and honorable and decent, and contrary to the teachings of my own faith tradition. Which is why, of course we should heed Harry's message and stand up for what is right!

RACISM'S UGLY SHADOW

A few years back an incident occurred in the small Louisiana town of Jena. It served to remind Americans that racism was still alive in the United States. It may be more subtle than a generation ago, but it's still with us.

The story of Jena begins with a tree on school property, which apparently was reserved for white students only. One day an African-American student got permission from the principal to sit there; that he needed permission to sit there suggests the systemic nature of racism. Later, after the student sat beneath the "white's only" tree, three nooses appeared as a sign of white displeasure with this breach of "etiquette." In the days that followed, a group of African-American students, unfortunately, turned to violence and responded by beating up a couple of the offending students. The local DA chose to charge these students in adult court, first with charges of attempted murder, and later with assault. While the conviction of one student was eventually overturned because he was convicted in the wrong venue, the events of Jena, Louisiana, have uncovered, much like Katrina, the realities of racism in our country.

My purpose here is not to delve into the charges or the counter charges of the Jena case, because the issues are too complex to get into here. But this series of events in a small Southern town gives us the opportunity to reflect on the shadow that racism continues to cast across our land.

We don't like to see ourselves as being racist, because we believe we've moved beyond that kind of activity and belief system. Jim Crow and the Klan, whites only rest rooms and lunch counters; all these reside in the dustbin of history. Unfortunately, racism remains with us four decades after the heyday of the Civil Rights movement. And racism isn't simply a Southern phenomenon – it infects the nation as a whole. It colors the immigration debate, national security, education, business, and even religion.

We use a number of terms interchangeably – terms like prejudice, discrimination, and racism. These words are related but not exactly the same. Prejudice is an attitude; discrimination is an action; racism takes both a step further. Racism has been defined by some as discriminatory acts based on ethnic or racial differences taken by people who have the power to exclude others. The key here is the "power to exclude." Racism isn't just individual attitudes, it's systemic. It's like a virus that invades the body, and which is therefore difficult to eradicate. Jim Crow may be dead, but his legacy remains – it is deeply embedded in our institutions and our government policies. Because it's systemic, it can perpetuate itself without our even recognizing it.

Sadly, racism is present in our religious institutions. If it weren't, then my denomination wouldn't find it necessary to address it from within. We recognize that while racism is a social evil, it is also a spiritual and theological problem. Racism denies the principle that we're all part of God's creation and reflect God's image – whether we're of Asian, African, European, Native American, Pacific Islander, or of mixed descent. We're all different in culture and ethnicity, but ultimately we're one family (and I say this as one who believes in evolution).

My denomination has called us as a church to be "anti-racist and pro-reconciling." The first calling is to root out all aspects of systemic racism in our churches – including that which infects our attitudes, our language, and our policies. In a sense this is the attempt to get rid of the log in our own eyes before removing the splinter in our neighbor's eye (Matthew 7:3). This will likely be an ongoing project.

From here we're called to become part of the solution – to seek reconciliation wherever possible in the broader community. We're called to raise our voices to defend the defenseless, to call into question injustice, and to bring people together. Ultimately, I've found that attitudes only change once we get to know each other better. That breaks down stereotypes, and when the stereotypes are removed, we see people as they really are – speaking theologically for a moment – God's children.

WELCOMING THE STRANGER?

Immigration Reform has long been the subject of debate in the nation's barber shops, pubs, grocery aisles, and break rooms. It has been discussed in blogs, opinion pages, chat rooms, by e-mail, and in the streets. It's one of those issues that simply won't go away, even though no one seems to agree on a solution. Although there's common agreement that something must be done, the question before us is whether there is any political will to get anything passed in the present environment.

Politics always makes dealing with contentious issues difficult, and with an unpopular President and a fairly evenly split Congress, compromise is difficult, especially with a presidential election cycle heating up. The debate will continue, even if reform waits to be enacted.

The facts in this debate are quite simple: Some twelve million people are said to be living in this country illegally, and every day that number increases. Most are here in search of the "American Dream" of a better life and a hopeful future. This is why immigrants have always come here. Of course there are those who come with malicious intent, but they're the minority. As it always has been, immigrant life is difficult – usually families are separated, immigrants live in cramped quarters, and most try to live under the radar lest they be sent home.

Although this is a political issue, it's also a moral one. It is, in fact, a debate over how we treat the stranger living in our midst. As the politicians debate, they hear a multitude of voices, all with different interests: the business community, agricultural interests, schools, health care providers, labor unions, and law enforcement. The proposed answers to the current dilemma range from the draconian to the lenient; from immediate deportation to providing a path to citizenship. When we listen to the myriad voices that are seeking our attention, we discover that there's really no consensus, no common will. But, doing nothing won't make the problem go away.

There's another voice – it's actually many different voices – that seeks our attention. That voice is the religious community, and like every segment of the population, it is not of one mind.

I can only speak for myself, but what I say reflects the teachings of my tradition. When I read the Hebrew Bible I find a stream of statements talking about how we should treat the alien. Most of these voices call on us to treat the stranger with respect and dignity. Don't oppress the alien in your midst, Jeremiah says on behalf of God, and I will be with you (Jeremiah 7:5-7). The Law encourages equal treatment of the stranger, and encourages farmers to leave out gleanings from the harvest for the poor and the alien dwelling in the country (Leviticus 23:22). Why, should they do this? The answer given is simple: "Love the stranger because once you were the stranger in Egypt" (Deuteronomy 10:18-19).

What then should I do as an American who is also a person of faith? The answer I seem to hear is this: you were once a stranger, so welcome the stranger who lives in your midst. Baptist theologian David Gushee writes:

> "Jesus calls us to love our neighbors as ourselves. He then makes clear that our 'neighbors' include not just family, friends and folk like us, but also strangers and enemies. Every person is my neighbor, whom I am called to love. The 'undocumented worker' or 'illegal alien' is my neighbor."

Now border security is necessary, but that's not the real issue. The real issue relates to those already here – and their families who haven't yet joined them. For now they live in the shadows and are easily used and abused.

If I listen to my faith, I hear a call to invite the stranger into the light of day so that they might live with dignity. They are, after all, my neighbor and are loved by God. If as the polls suggest, we're a nation of the faithful, then surely we must consider carefully this voice and seek to a way forward that's humane and compassionate. These are our brothers and our sisters and members of a common human family, created in the image of God.

A CUP OF WATER FOR AN ALIEN

For years we have heard calls for immigration reform. In part because of a lack of movement on the issue at the Federal level, some states have taken matters into their own hands, imposing rather draconian solutions that can lead to racial/ethnic profiling and harassment. Not since the Reagan Administration have meaningful responses to immigration issues been undertaken, and so millions of people, including children find themselves in legal limbo, even as questions abound as to the impact of undocumented people n the American economy and the nation's social and cultural systems.

Polls certainly suggest that immigration is an issue of concern, with questions of security complicating what was once considered an economic or cultural issue. These polls also suggest that Americans are sharply divided over the issue. That there are such sharp divisions over immigration shouldn't surprise us. Although we are a nation of immigrants, there has long been an anti-immigrant sentiment in America. Think of the Klan and the Know-Nothing Party of the 19th Century. Back then the targets were African-Americans, Irish, Italian, and Jewish, but as time wore on others were added to the list. Perhaps you remember the sentiment as it played out in the movie *Gangs of New York*.

America has a tradition of opening its doors to immigrants. My ancestors came from England, Scotland, Ireland, Germany, and Holland in search of a new life and new opportunities. They responded to the message engraved on the Statue of Liberty:

Give me your tired, your poor,
Your huddled masses yearning to breathe free,
The wretched refuse of your teeming shore.
Send these, the homeless, tempest-tost to me,
I lift my lamp beside the golden door!

Of course, the welcome mat has been more freely extended to some than to others.

That something must be done to fix a broken immigration system is without question, but the debates show that there is no easy or perfect solution. As history demonstrates, building walls does little to keep determined migrants out and criminalizing acts of charity seems not just un-American, but inhumane. Besides, there are economic issues – we've become dependent on immigrant labor (whether legal or not) to work our farms, clean our homes and hotels, cook our food, mow our lawns, and clean our houses. Most of the eleven million "illegals" living here, work hard, hoping they can better their lives. That was the goal of my ancestors as well.

When Roman Catholic Cardinal Roger Mahoney of Los Angeles issued a much criticized statement that said that the Catholic Church would continue offering compassionate services to illegal immigrants even if the practice is outlawed by the government, many called this statement un-American. That may be true, but I remember a group of Christians who told the governing officials that they must obey God rather than human authorities (Acts 4:18-21).

Cardinal Mahoney's words echo biblical traditions that call for God's people to care for the alien and the foreigner among them. The book of Leviticus says: "when an alien resides with you in your land, you shall not oppress the alien. The alien who resides with you shall be to you as the citizen among you; you shall love the alien as yourself, for you were aliens in the land of Egypt: I am the Lord your God" (Leviticus 19:33-34). As we debate immigration reform, perhaps these words will offer us some vital guidelines.

While security is certainly an issue of great concern, fear must not be the engine that drives immigration reform. With few illegals coming here for malicious reasons, let's remember the call to care for the neighbor in need. Besides, it's short-sighted to deny the alien, whether legal or not, education and medical care. One faith-based organization that has tackled this issue head on is Humane Borders, a Tucson based organization that not only advocates for immigration reform, it provides water stations in the desert. In spite of walls and border patrols, people keep migrating north, many of whom make it across the border only to die of thirst in the searing desert heat. But, a cup of water, a very biblical image, can save a life. For more information about this ministry, check their website: http://www.humaneborders.org/. As Deuteronomy reminds us: "You shall love the stranger, for you were strangers in the land of Egypt" (Deuteronomy 10:19).

Remembering Again the Holocaust

The Holocaust stands out among the most horrific atrocities of human history. The very word conjures up images of death in our minds, but six decades after the liberation of the Nazi death camps, those images and stories have begun to fade from our memories. We know that the Holocaust (*Shoah* in Hebrew) was a Nazi effort to extinguish the lives of those they deemed undesirable, but we give this little thought as we live our out daily lives.

Although there were many others, including Gypsies and the mentally disabled that faced the Nazi's genocidal mania, it was the Jews who bore the brunt of this horror. By most counts, six million Jews died between 1938 and 1945, with more than a million dying in the Nazi gas chambers. There are those who continue to deny the Holocaust, including the current president of Iran, but in spite of their efforts the evidence speaks for itself. Auschwitz, Dachau, Birkenau, Buchenwald, Mathausen, Neuengamme, Ravensbrueck, Sachsenhausen, Belzec, Sobibor, and Treblinka are names and places that are seared or should be seared into the minds of us all. Just as important for our remembrances are the voices of the survivors. Their stories are powerful reminders of what happened in Europe during the early 1940s. These aren't stories easily heard, because they witness to the fact that humans are capable of abominable acts.

Jewish history is replete with stories of pogroms, ghettoes, discrimination, vandalism, and death. In this case, what came to be known as the Final Solution was instigated in the name of nationalism and racial purity. It was given further support, unfortunately, by Christians whose theology encouraged then to seek revenge for Jesus' death. They were, in their own minds, exacting blood guilt. But no matter who was involved in his death, Jesus from the cross offered forgiveness and amnesty. No blood guilt need be exacted. Ironically, if Jesus had lived in 1940's Germany he would have been its victim, for there is no denying that he was and is and always will be Jewish.

The 27th of Nissan in the Jewish calendar is known as *Yom HaShoah* or Holocaust Remembrance Day. It is a national holiday in Israel, but it is also day for Jews around the world to remember the ones who gave their lives and to honor those who survived.

Yom HaShoah is a day of mourning and remembrance for the Jewish community, but I'm not Jewish. In many ways, it's not my place to speak of such things, and by speaking of it, I speak as much out of ignorance as knowledge. Still, as Martin Niemoller, a German theologian and opponent of the Nazi program, stated so eloquently, if I don't stand up for others, who will stand for me when my enemies come. So, today I choose to speak in honor and in remembrance of those who died and those who survived. I also speak in honor of the many who risked their lives to rescue Jews, for their example spurs me on to action.

I've had the privilege of participating in several services of remembrance. I've watched as survivors and the children and grandchildren of victims and survivors lit candles in memory of those who died. I've also heard stories from the lips of survivors. These are stories we must hear. Some are inspiring while others bring tears to our eyes. Unfortunately, the ranks of the survivors and the rescuers are being depleted by time and death. But their stories need to be heard, remembered, and treasured so that such a thing might not happen again.

We know, of course, that genocide did not die with the liberation of Auschwitz or the death of Hitler. It continues to live on in other parts of the world. Even prior to the Holocaust there was the Armenian Genocide and more recently we heard the stories of Rwanda, and now we hear of Darfur. When the 27th of Nissan comes each year, may we stand together, whether Jew or non-Jew, in solidarity with our human brothers and sisters who face death daily simply for who they are. May our voices be heard, so that the march of death might be stopped.

"It Still Takes a Village to Raise a Child"

Hillary Clinton, then First Lady, quoted an African proverb and opined that "it takes a village to raise a child." Her word of advice was countered by claims that strong families, not the village, are we need. Families are important, but the point of the proverb is still difficult to refute, for even the strongest families can't raise their children alone. It takes a community committed and willing to provide children with a safe and nurturing environment, one that offers quality educations, opportunities to explore one's creative side or participate in sports. It takes families, government, non-profits, religious organizations, businesses, and yes, law enforcement to provide such an environment.

Most communities face difficult challenges, including gangs and drugs that threaten the wholeness of the community. Though families play a significant role in responding to these challenges, they can't protect their children forever. If we think that the solution is simply increased support for law enforcement – to suppress or keep at bay the gangs and drug traffickers – then we are naïve. Law enforcement plays an important role, but it doesn't get at the root issues.

Gangs are successful, because they offer young people a sense of purpose and belonging. They are like tribes that offer an alternative to the village (which includes the family). Though gangs are often criminal enterprises, for many kids, especially those who lack strong families or suffer low self-esteem, are lonely or struggle in school, the gang, they become a family. Like any tribe, gangs enforce a sense of loyalty and provide a code of honor. To the outsider they may appear to be just a bunch of thugs, but gangs are not anarchists. They are tightly knit organizations that give order to the often chaotic lives of the gang members. Loyalty and honor are prized above all else, so if you offend my honor, my tribe will defend me – sometimes to the death. Violence is the means of expanding gang turf, but more importantly it defends the honor of the gang its members. In this, it mimics the nation-state, which expands its borders, and defends its honor.

I'm not an expert on gangs, but I believe that if the village (the community as a whole and not just the government) has the will, it can marshal its resources and offer clear and positive responses. It will take all segments of the community – business, government, schools, religious institutions, non-profit organizations, and of course families. The responses must be more than diversions or entertaining programs; it will take a multi-level approach that includes investment in our public schools, in vocational education, in mentoring opportunities and internships, along with increased support for music education (both instrumental and vocal), theater, the arts, and athletics. These kinds of programs build leaders and offer young people a sense of purpose and give meaning to their lives. Programs that teach young people how to resolve conflicts nonviolently and reinforce virtues such as respect, tolerance, and justice will be crucial. The community will also need to offer counseling programs that can aid young people who have become enticed by drugs and gangs to help them find a way out. All of this takes money, but in the long run it's a lot cheaper than building prisons. If the village is going to respond effectively then it must start its work when children are still young. High school may not be too late, but the longer we wait the more difficult it becomes.

If the image of the village still seems foreign, then perhaps the image of the extended family will work. Jesus defined the family broadly, family including in his family all who followed him. So perhaps we can think of ourselves as a big and very diverse family that is able to expand and include, support and be compassionate. It's the kind of family where everyone is an aunt or uncle, grandmother or grandfather, who is willing to guide and mentor, teach and encourage. In a mobile society like ours, our children need an extended family – perhaps a faith community that is willing to embrace a young person in need of family. Then perhaps, none of them will fall through the cracks. Yes, it takes a village or maybe a great big family, to face down the challenges to the future of our children.

CAN THERE EVER BE PEACE IN THE MIDDLE EAST?

When I wrote this column the newscasts were abuzz with stories of death and destruction. Lebanon was burning and Hezbollah rockets rained down on northern Israeli towns. In many ways there wasn't anything new about this current news cycle. For much of the last half century, Israel, the Palestinian (Occupied) Territories, and Lebanon have been the scene of war and regular acts of violence. That Jerusalem means "city of peace" carries great irony.

Who really knows when a cycle of violence begins, but the intensity of that particular cycle coincided with the killing and kidnapping of Israeli soldiers by a Hamas aligned group, which led in turn to harsh Israeli retaliation. A northern "front" opened when Hezbollah guerillas based in southern Lebanon crossed the border and kidnapped two more Israeli soldiers. This act of aggression led to a massive Israeli response that has laid waste to much of Lebanon, threatening the viability of an already fragile democracy. All the while, the world stands by watching the violence escalate and the death toll on civilians, whether Israeli, Palestinian, or Lebanese climb. As an ineffectual UN attempts to find a solution, the United States chose to remain on the sidelines, leaving it to others to find that solution.

As a Christian I have a personal stake in this region. This is, after all, the land where Jesus walked. Too often we think of this as simply a Jewish/Muslim conflict, but in doing so we forget the ancient Christian community that lives in the region – though these numbers have been greatly diminished by emigration during the last half century. Even though I've never been to the region, I remain connected, because it plays such a central role in my own faith story.

I join with Christians, Jews, and Muslims, Israelis, Palestinians, Jordanians, and Lebanese who wish to see a permanent end to the violence. Peace can be had, but people on all sides must choose a different course of action. The National Council of Churches issued a statement that called on our government to join with the world's other governments in working to bring an end to the hostilities and then engage in the difficult work of resolving the deeply rooted issues that have prolonged the violence. It also called on all the parties in the region to immediately end the hostilities and look to non-violent strategies of engagement. But this document doesn't just speak to governments; it speaks to the religious communities in the region and beyond. To the religious communities closest to the violence it calls on them to advocate for and teach the way of peace. Finally, it calls on member churches to pray "for all those who have suffered and died as a result of this violence, and their families and communities, and to engage in humanitarian and advocacy actions for peace."

The path forward will be difficult and fraught with dangerous roadblocks. Many don't want peace. Hamas and its allies (including Iran) are committed to the destruction of Israel. A small coterie of Israelis, together with their evangelical supporters, look to the restoration of greater Israel. Either course will lead to the displacement or death of millions. It's a course that the vast majority of Israelis and most Palestinians don't support, but there are enough partisans to keep the conflict hot for the foreseeable future. In the meantime innocent civilians, Jewish, Muslim, and Christian suffer loss of life and property.

We've reached an impasse – the chosen course of action isn't working and it never has. There is some hope in the course suggested by the National Council of Churches, which includes a call on each of us to do our part. We can start by being informed about the conflict and the parties who are involved in it. We can make our voices heard in the public square, and we can pray that peace will prevail. Perhaps you, like me, feel that your loyalties are challenged by this crisis. My Jewish friends want me to back Israel, while Muslim friends encourage my support of the Palestinian cause. It's truly a complex issue, but I'll continue my prayers that peace will come to the city of Peace and to its neighbors.

THE VALUE OF WORK

The Bible says: "In all toil there is profit, but mere talk leads only to poverty" (Proverbs 14:23), and Ben Franklin said: "Early to bed and early to rise, makes a man healthy, wealthy, and wise." Both sayings seem appropriate for Labor Day weekend, because both affirm the value of labor. That's also the point of Ralph Waldo Emerson's adage that "the reward of a thing well done, is to have done it." The point of these sayings is: It doesn't matter what we do, whether we're building a house, planting a garden, harvesting a field, writing a book, or acing a test, when we see the product of our work we can take pride in our accomplishment.

Work is good, but reality can put a damper on our celebration. Sometimes work is dehumanizing, dangerous, or just plain back-breaking. The only benefit of such work is the wage it pays, which too often is a mere pittance.

I count myself fortunate that I enjoy my job and that it pays a decent wage. Though I've worked hard and spent many years in school, I've also had my share of breaks. For too many Americans "work" isn't something they enjoy or take pride in; it's simply what they do to survive. So, work may be good, but not all work is good for you. That's why the labor movement arose and why our government has passed minimum wage, children's labor, and safety laws. These are laws that should be celebrated and strengthened, not weakened.

It's likely that there are many in the labor force who face a different problem. Their work isn't necessarily back-breaking or dehumanizing, but it has its liabilities. It's well documented that work is an idol for many. We work, not to survive, but because it consumes us. It's the reason we live, and it crowds out everything else from our lives. It's become the modern American dilemma, because in spite of all our modern conveniences Americans are busier working than ever. Researchers say that we have 40% less free time today than when I was growing up in the 1970s, with the average American working a month longer per year than thirty years ago. We may be more productive, but what's the cost to our families, the community, and our relationship with God, all of which are sacrificed to our workaholism.

Unfortunately, many Americans have also discovered that our economy requires us to work day and night to achieve the American dream. That dream isn't the castle on the hill but the 3 bedroom ranch-style house we grew up in. Though our identity may be caught up in our jobs, sometimes this idol is not of our own choosing.

Psychiatrist Karl Menninger wrote that "Those who rhapsodize about the joy of labor are likely to be persons who are not obliged to do much of it." Menninger's statement is worthy of consideration, because whether it's a matter of choice or not, when work becomes an idol, it keeps us from being responsible spouses, parents, and citizens. My employment is important, but it's not my most important calling in life. Putting food on the table and shelter over our heads requires that we "have a job." Sometimes that job gives us pleasure and a sense of purpose, but it can also become dehumanizing and destructive – either to us or to our relationships.

Work is good, but life transcends our jobs. As a Christian, I'm reminded that my first calling or vocation is to be a follower of Jesus Christ, and as such I've been called to love and serve my neighbor. As part of this service to God and neighbor, I'm invited to engage in labor that will provide food and shelter for me and my family. From what I earn I can also contribute to the welfare of others who share this world of ours. I may be employed, but my divinely given vocation is to be a blessing to others. It's good that we celebrate the value of labor, but we must keep our priorities straight and work to make sure that labor in our country is safe, secure, and humane. While not every job will have the same intrinsic value, every job can be life affirming.

THE SANCTITY OF LIFE – WHAT IS IT?

With all the chocolate eggs and bunnies, along with those marshmallow chicks, filling Easter baskets, the children will today be all atwitter from their sugar induced high. As a secular and commercial holiday, Easter celebrates spring's arrival in festive ways.

Even in its more commercial expressions, Easter celebrates life. As a Christian celebration, Easter is the most important day of the year. It is, in fact, the pivotal moment in our religious life, for it celebrates God's no to death in the resurrection of Jesus. And so, whether you take this doctrine literally or metaphorically, it stands for Christians as God's no to death and yes to life.

Looking at life through the lens of Easter, we discover how precious it is. Indeed, to use a politically charged word, Easter proclaims the "sanctity of life." It's unfortunate that this phrase, like the equally politicized word "pro-life," has come to mean only a concern for "life before birth." Shouldn't life's sanctity apply not just to life in the womb, but include all of life, especially that life existing between birth and death?

"Reverence for life," theologian Jürgen Moltmann writes, "always begins with respect for weaker life, vulnerable life." And that would include "the poor, the sick, and the defenseless." It also includes concern for non-human life. Regard for nature considers "the weaker animal and plant species, the life of which is at present condemned to extinction because of human barbarism" (Moltmann, 49-50). If we're to be truly pro-life, then we must expand the category considerably.

The Psalmist says that the earth belongs to the Lord, along with all who dwell in it (Psalm 24:1). Although Genesis does suggest that God takes a special interest in his human creation, it doesn't appear that God is concerned only about humankind. It is all of life that stands in the purview of God.

So, what does it mean to be pro-life? In my thinking, to be pro-life would include concern about war and its impact on life.

Christians often talk about just war, but with so many "civilians" dying or being displaced by modern war, it has become increasingly difficult to consider any war just. War may sometimes be necessary, but it's difficult to justify it on the basis of faith.

To be pro-life is to be concerned about the environment, because the environment is our habitation, and clean air and clean water are essential for healthy living. It would also include concern about poverty, because poverty undermines the quality of life and even the longevity of life. Indeed, if one wishes to reduce abortions, it would seem appropriate to focus on reducing poverty. Finally, to be pro-life is to be concerned about affordable and effective health care. AIDS, cancer, diabetes, any number of infectious diseases, and more are scourges on life. They can and do cut lives short. And with so many uninsured in this country, families must often choose between food and shelter or health care, because they can't afford both. I could continue the list, but I don't have space to do so. But, if we wish to claim the mantle of being "pro-life," then we should be concerned about what happens between the time of birth and the time of death.

For me, Easter is about the resurrection of Jesus and its witness to the sanctity of all life. It's a call to be concerned about matters of life and death and a call to action that includes not just Christians, but everyone, religious or not. Because a true solution requires government involvement, it will of necessity become a matter of politics. After all, it's the politicians who send young men and women into battle and decide what a minimum wage is. They decide how medical care will be distributed and how to fund education. They pass the laws that will protect our water supply, or they won't.

Although politicians will of necessity play a leading role, our nation's political system gives us the right and responsibility to choose our leaders and hold them accountable. On this Easter Sunday, let's all, whether Christian or not, commit ourselves to cherishing life, especially that life which is the most vulnerable, whether human or not. This, I think would be in tune with the message of the resurrection.

LIFE IN THE BALANCE – THE STEM CELL DEBATE

Scientific and technological advances over the last century, especially those in the medical and bio-technology fields, have been a blessing. Life expectancy is reaching once unimaginable levels, and diseases that were once killers are now simply nuisances that can usually be prevented or at least controlled with medication. But, sometimes these advancements outstrip our ability to reflect ethically on their ramifications and consequences. As the Nazis proved, just because you *can* do something doesn't mean you *should*.

Embryonic stem cell research is one of those issues that's been caught up in these kinds of debates. While the vast majority of Americans support embryonic stem-cell research, a vocal opposition has been raising ethical and moral questions that have stymied efforts to fund research at the federal level. In 2006, when President Bush issued his first presidential veto and turned back a bipartisan bill to fund research, he argued that the destruction of embryos (even frozen ones that would be discarded if not implanted) crossed a moral boundary he was unwilling to support. This occurred despite polls suggesting that approximately 70% of Americans support this research. With a ban on federal funds in place, many states, including California, have tried to fill the gap with state funding. Research is also being pursued overseas, but at least at the federal level the United States has opted out of the race to find the next "great cure." That veto delayed federal funding, but bipartisan efforts to find ways of funding the research continued to be pursued in Congress, and the ban was finally reversed by President Obama.

As for the science involved, the National Institute of Health's website defines a stem cell as a cell with "the remarkable potential to develop into many different cell types in the body. Serving as a sort of repair system for the body, they can theoretically divide without limit to replenish other cells, as long as the person or animal is still alive." It's believed by a majority of scientists in this field that embryonic stem cells offer the best hope of finding cures for many of the scourges that plague human life, including Parkinson's and Alzheimer's diseases. The recently trumpeted news that amniotic cells might provide a promising source of stem-cell lines has been jumped on by opponents of embryonic stem-cell research, who argue that these lines should substitute for the more controversial embryonic lines. The reality is that even the researcher who made the discovery says that amniotic lines are a supplement not a replacement for the embryonic lines. Therefore, if we wish to find hoped for cures, we still must continue research on embryonic lines.

Opponents of embryonic stem cell research liken it to abortion, believing that if life begins at conception, then even frozen embryos represent human life and deserve protection. Therefore, the central moral/ethical questions turn on our definition of life's beginning point. Still, if the embryos under consideration are leftovers from *in vitro* fertilization efforts and will be discarded if not used, are we really talking about human life? Besides, if this research could possibly benefit untold numbers of people, wouldn't this be the most pro-life action one could pursue? A majority of Americans would answer this second question in the affirmative.

Much of the opposition to the research is religiously based, but the religious community isn't of one mind on this issue. In fact, the normative religious texts are largely silent on this and many other scientific questions. Neither the Bible (Jewish or Christian versions) nor the Qur'an speak directly to this issue, and so we're left debating broader issues such as when life begins and whether people who might benefit from potential treatments should have priority over the potentiality of these embryos. Many of us who have watched Alzheimer's and Parkinson's rob friends and loved ones of dignity and life, have concluded that we should pursue these promising treatments.

Still, the question of when life begins nags at us, and in this our religious texts don't offer conclusive guidance. The Qur'an argues strenuously for the preservation of life, but it also distinguishes between potential life and life itself. The same is true of the

Hebrew Bible, while the Christian New Testament is silent. I can't say with certainty when life begins, but my moral inclination is to protect life wherever possible. That being said, if embryos are destined to degrade or be destroyed before fulfilling their potentiality, then surely it would be the moral thing to use them to pursue research that could lead to important cures and treatments. This, it would seem to me, is the moral imperative of our day.

WE NEED TO TALK

Whenever someone says "We need to talk," we know the topic of conversation is going to be difficult. It's natural to try to avoid conflict, especially when we fear that tempers might flair and relationships will be broken. We say: "Let sleeping dogs lie," and "What they don't know won't hurt them." From an early age we learn what's appropriate for polite discussion and what isn't.

It's this sensibility that lies behind the military's "Don't ask, Don't tell" policy regarding homosexuals serving in the military, which was finally reversed in 2011. The policy was enacted because homosexuality is a controversial issue in our culture – and so if we don't ask, we don't have to deal with the question of sexual orientation. Thus, if you're gay or lesbian and serving in the military, it's best to stay in the closet.

What is official military policy has become unofficial policy in much of our society, including our religious communities. A Baptist pastor friend of mine lost his job because of a pictorial directory. Although his church has been welcoming gays and lesbians for years, a group in the church balked at the decision to put gay and lesbian couples together in directory pictures – acknowledging their partnership. As long as people stay in the closet, we feel comfortable with the policy of "don't ask, don't tell."

Our culture's discomfort with the question of sexual orientation is wrapped up with our equal discomfort in talking about sexuality in general. This is true in spite of the fact that our culture is saturated by it. Consider the adage: "Sex sells." If it weren't true, ad agencies and TV producers wouldn't bother with it. Our fears keep us from talking. When it comes to sex education in our schools, many opponents say this should be a family matter. But the truth is families often aren't up to the challenge. If we have difficulties discussing sexuality in a frank and open way, it's no surprise that we find the topic of sexual orientation to be problematic.

The shooting death in 2006 of Lawrence King, a 15 year old Oxnard junior high school student, at the hands of a fellow student served as a wakeup call to many of us living along the Central Coast of California. The victim had revealed to his peers that he was gay, a revelation that led to taunts, teasing, and threats – does that sound surprising? It appears that Larry may have responded on occasion to these threats by flirting, which only made the problem worse. One of those students involved in this situation was Brandon McInearny, a bright young man who came from a broken and violent home. Both young men had issues they struggled with, and in the end this was a fatal combination for both of them. We wonder if this would have happened if our society was better equipped to handle differences in sexual or gender orientation. I don't know all the details – including possible efforts by the school to mediate the problem beforehand. But, we as a society must recognize that our discomfort with the issue prevents our young people from knowing how to properly deal with differences. In a society that still considers violence to be a legitimate means of expression, when we're unwilling to talk about deeply divisive issues in our society, violence can and will happen. In this case, one teen is dead and the other faces the possibility of life in prison. Whatever the troubles of their past lives, now neither has a future.

I understand why we find it difficult to talk about the issue. There are significant differences of understanding about homosexuality – whether it's a choice or not, and whether or not it's a moral issue. I understand the question well, because before my brother came out I believed homosexuality to be a choice and immoral. Since that time, I've wrestled with the question and have changed my mind. But, knowing how divisive the question is, I'm still hesitant to raise the issue in the church. In our church we're welcoming but we're still not sure what that means. I think that's true of much of our society at this moment. But if we're going to bring an end to the violence against the Larry Kings and Matthew Shepherds of our world, we need to start talking in earnest.

SAYING NO TO VIOLENCE

The news of April 16, 2007 stunned the nation; not news that nearly 200 people died in Iraq, but that thirty-three students and faculty members lay dead from a mass-murder-suicide at Virginia Tech. It hit many of us hard, because we expect college campuses to be safe havens for learning and transitions in life.

In the days that followed we learned the who, the how, and the possible why. We learned that one victim was a Holocaust survivor who had died trying to save his students. We watched video of the perpetrator of this violence declare his anger at the world in an attempt to justify his turn to violence. We also heard pundits and politicians debate the merits of gun ownership and gun regulation. All of this was mixed together with a national sense of grief and continued disbelief.

But, why are we so shocked? Americans have an almost voyeuristic interest in violence. It dominates our TV shows, video games, music, and movies. Characters like Rambo, the Terminator, and Dirty Harry are heroic archetypes, and slasher movies draw big crowds.

As I watched the Oscar winning movie *The Departed* not long afterward, I found it to be a character study of our trust in the utility of violence. Even though almost everyone in the film dies in the end, the message here seems to be that it takes a bit of violence to get ahead in life. And when Osama bin Laden brought down buildings in New York we promised "shock and awe" in response. Responding to this act of violence, our leaders talked of pre-emptive war and later we heard defenses of torture in the name of security (from fellow Christians at that).

As for this young man who took the lives of his fellow students and their teachers, a couple of things stood out. He fits the profile of recent mass killers – He was a loner, friendless, and angry at the world for perceived injustices. He was – to put it mildly – alienated from the world in which he lived. This mental state was compounded by the hours he apparently spent playing ultra-violent video games that stoked his anger. While I know that only a few who play such games or watch violent movies will commit horrible acts of violence, these culturally approved expressions of violence may have more of an effect than many of us are willing to acknowledge. Given the right psychological trigger and the all too readily available tools of violence, perhaps we might explode into violence, even as this one student did. Indeed, such acts happen every day in our nation, even on the streets of our own community.

Bobby Kennedy said, in a speech entitled "On the Mindless Menace of Violence," just months before he would die of an assassin's bullet:

> "Whenever any American's life is taken by another American unnecessarily - whether it is done in the name of the law or in the defiance of the law, by one man or a gang, in cold blood or in passion, in an attack of violence or in response to violence - whenever we tear at the fabric of the life which another man has painfully and clumsily woven for himself and his children, the whole nation is degraded."

Indeed, our lives have been degraded by acts of violence at home and abroad.

As I consider the violence that colors our existence, I'm led to something Jesus said: "You have heard that it was said to those of ancient times, 'You shall not murder'; . . . But I say to you that if you are angry with your brother or sister, you will be liable to judgment." (Matthew 5: 21-22).

Seemingly every religious tradition has voices that council war and voices that council peace. And of course there's often a bit of hypocrisy going on as members of different religions point fingers at each other. Since I'm a Christian I find it ironic that fellow Christians point fingers at Muslims and point to passages of the Qur'an and say, "theirs is a religion of violence," when we seem to ignore what Jesus says about loving our enemies. Yes, and then there is Christian history itself, which is full of violence. No one, it seems, is immune to the grip of violence.

But this needn't be the way the things are. Indeed, may the events of April 16, 2007, both in Blacksburg and in Baghdad, lead us along a path away from the path of violence.

IS TORTURE JUSTIFIABLE?

People driven by fear can engage in the most heinous of acts. They're like a cornered animal who lashes out at anyone or anything that's nearby. Whether it's communism, crime, or perhaps terrorism, if fear is the driving force, we might even try to justify torture. It's unlikely that we'd use the term. A euphemism, "enhanced interrogation techniques," would be preferable, but the action is the same.

During a presidential primary debate in 2008, candidates were asked how they'd respond to a scenario seeming taken from a "24" script. No one gave a nod to torture, but several leading candidates came very close. The question is: how far are willing to go to protect ourselves in the name of national security? This isn't a hypothetical question. It's common knowledge that the George W. Bush administration sought to find ways around the Geneva Conventions, which they deemed quaint and too limiting in this conflict of ours. Then we learned of the abuses at Abu Ghraib. Even if these weren't ordered from on high, our attempts at evading longstanding treaty obligations give at least tacit permission for such activities.

With torture there are two different issues to be considered. One has to do with the effectiveness of the actions in question, and the other relates to its morality. The argument for such coercive techniques such as water boarding or sleep deprivation is that they produce information that saves lives, and we all want to save lives. But many experts in the field of interrogation believe that these techniques are largely ineffective – wouldn't you say anything to free yourself from pain. Just tell them what they want to hear! One of those experts is Chuck Blanchard, a former General Counsel to the United States Army, who wrote on his blog: "For decades, it was the official position of the U.S. Government that torture (defined to include the techniques approved by the current Administration) was counter-productive, wrong, and a violation of both domestic and international law (http://aguyinthepew.

blogspot.com/2007/05/thoughts-on-torture.html).” The commanding general in Iraq at the time and now Director of the CIA, David Petraeus, seems to concur and suggests that much of the information gathered in this way is of little use to them. One reason why the military has resisted such techniques is that they could easily be used against our troops – and if we use them how can we tell others not to use them?

Such is the utilitarian response, but what of the moral response? The idea that we should use whatever means necessary (short of torture, of course) has a certain resonance with many our nation, but there's significant opposition from within the religious community to this sentiment. For a response, there's no better place to start than the statement produced by the *National Religious Coalition against Torture*. It reads:

> Torture violates the basic dignity of the human person that all religions, in their highest ideals, hold dear. It degrades everyone involved – policy-makers, perpetrators, and victims. It contradicts our nation's most cherished ideals. Any policies that permit torture and inhumane treatment are shocking and morally intolerable.

One of the persons involved in drafting this statement is David Gushee, an Evangelical philosopher and ethicist, who has written extensively on this subject. Among the reasons why we should reject the use of torture, Gushee offers these five responses:

> Torture violates the intrinsic dignity of the human being, made in the image of God.
>
> 1. Torture mistreats the vulnerable and thus violates the demands of public justice.
> 2. Authorizing any forms of torture trusts government too much.
> 3. Torture invites the dehumanizing of the torturer.

   4.   Torture erodes the character of the nation
       that tortures.

Morally, torture not only dehumanizes the victim, it affects the moral bearing of the torturer and the nation that authorizes it.

If, as my faith tradition teaches, we're called to love our neighbors and do good and not harm, then where does torture or even enhanced interrogation methods fit? Jesus tells us to even love our enemies; so if Christianity has influenced this nation at all, this command precludes torture or actions akin to torture. And if that passage doesn't get your attention, then perhaps this one will: "Remember those who are in prison, as though you were in prison with them; those who are being tortured, as though you yourselves were being tortured" (Hebrews 13:3 NRSV). The biblical writer suggests that we put ourselves in the shoes of the one being tortured and then decide what's appropriate.

A WORD ABOUT JAILS

During budget crises, politicians must make difficult choices, including what should be done with funding public safety services. Such a crisis has long faced the state of California, which has a prison system that lacks sufficient capacity to house the number of prisoners already in custody. When budget realities collide with insufficient capacity, the state faces the prospect of either setting prisoners free or cutting other important services – including education and health care.

As with any politically difficult issue, this one is complex. We understand the need for prisons to house those people who would pose a danger to society. But, ultimately the issue is much bigger than the need for more prisons and beds. The question is: Why is there such a need? It's true that the population in our nation and in our state continues to grow, which might explain the problem of increasing numbers of prisoners. However, crime rates have been on the decline for some time. Besides this, a more troubling question pertains to the fact that the percentage of Americans on probation, in jail, or in prison is higher than in any other developed nation.

In doing a bit of research on this issue, I discovered that in 2005 there were more than seven million Americans in jail, prison, or on parole. That's 3.2% of the U.S. population, and the numbers are steadily increasing. From 1995 to 2005, the rate of incarceration grew at an annual rate of 3.3%. California, by itself, has the third largest penal system in the world, and taken by itself the rest of the nation is in the top two.

Despite the fact that we've been building jails and prisons like mad, we just can't seem to keep up with the need. Indeed, the current bed capacity for California prisons stands at around 88,000, but the number of incarcerated persons is running at around 170,000 – that's 186.3% of their design capacity. While many prisoners are dangerous felons, significant numbers are there due to drug-related arrests (21%). Over the past quarter century,

California's prison population has increased 554%, an increase partly explained by more mandatory and longer sentences, the three-strike law, and the rate of recidivism, especially among those jailed for drug-related offenses.

All of these numbers are staggering, and they produce a significant drag on the state and federal budgets, because keeping people in prison isn't cheap. The State of California spends over $7 billion per year on its Department of Corrections, and while that number is much smaller than the $55 billion or so spent on the state's education budget, considering the numbers of people involved this number is very significant. The amount spent per prisoner is significantly higher than what is spent per pupil, and what we spend on the state's correctional system is ultimately money that could have been spent on what is an increasingly under-funded education system.

Like anyone, I'm concerned about public safety. And yes, there's a place for jails and prisons, at least as long as human beings are prone to violence and chicanery. Still, these numbers must be addressed, and in addressing them, we must move beyond the idea that building more jails and prisons will solve the problem. Something must be done to address the underlying issues that have feed this problem.

As we consider a solution, I'm reminded that claiming the mantle of the Jewish prophet Isaiah (Luke 4:18), Jesus stated clearly that he came to set the prisoners free. In considering this statement of purpose, I believe that the solutions lie beyond beefing up the penal system. It lies in education and in jobs. It requires us to address matters of poverty and the growing problem of drug abuse in our state and nation. The answers to these kinds of questions won't be found in the incarceration of our fellow citizens. Ultimately, the solution to this issue will be found within the community, in our willingness to work together to solve the underlying problems of society. Because having one of the largest penal systems in the world isn't anything to be proud of.

CONSIDERING THE HOMELESS

"Foxes have holes and birds of the air have nests; but the Son of Man has nowhere to lay his head" (Matthew 8:20). This is Jesus' description of his own living situation. If we take this passage at face value, it suggests that he was homeless.

A follower of Jesus, I've never known true homelessness. Living for a time in the Pasadena YMCA is as close to being homeless as I've ever been. After paying the first months rent, I had less than a $100 in my pocket and no job. My situation was difficult, but there were prospects for a job and a family who would have helped – even if they lived out-of-state. As brief as my stay on the edge of homelessness was, it gave me a glimpse into what it must be like to not know where the next meal will come from or not have a roof over one's head. It was only a glimpse, but for many it's a daily reality.

People are homeless for different reasons. Though incomprehensible to many of us, some of the homeless choose to live on the streets. But there are many others, the vast majority, who didn't choose this life. Some are there due to mental illness or drug and alcohol issues. Others have landed on the streets or in shelters because of economic factors – including health related bills. Each has his or her own story to tell, and many of the stories are heartbreaking – especially when children are involved.

In many cases the reality of homelessness is a hidden issue, but the reality is that living among us are the poor, the needy, the sick, and those without adequate and affordable housing. It's not someone else's problem to address, it's a problem the entire community must address. To better understand the issue, I did a little online research. I ran across HUD's "Annual Homeless Assessment Report to Congress" (February 2007), which estimates that between February 1 and April 30, 2005, there was a daily average of 334, 744 people living in homeless shelters, while another 338, 781 people were living unsheltered. Of those in shelters, 66% were individuals, while another 34% involved an adult with at least one child. Another study estimated that over a 5-year period upwards of 8 million Americans experienced at least one night of homelessness. These numbers are significant enough that they should get our attention.

Finding a solution to the problem won't be easy. It will take money and political will. Religious communities, like the one I pastor, will have a role to play in this effort, but ultimately it will take the community as a whole – government, businesses, schools, non-profits, mental health, and medical providers – working together to find a solution. Ignoring the problem won't make it go away, and as a follower of one who once was homeless, I know I must open my eyes to the problem and join in the effort to make a difference.

LISTENING FOR NATURE'S VOICE

Global warming, Al Gore says, is an inconvenient truth. We are seeing patterns of climate change that include changes in migration patterns, a shrinking Arctic ice pack, huge ice sheets breaking free from Antarctica, and the shrinking of glaciers world-wide. Some of this may be due to natural cycles, but there's also clear evidence that human actions are speeding up the process. Besides climate change, we've seen holes appear in the ozone layer, the disappearance of wet lands and rain forests, and an increase in pollution in all its forms. While industrialization has improved life, that improvement has come with unfortunate side effects. Finding the right balance won't be easy, and it likely will prove costly, but the alternative is leaving an uninhabitable world to our descendents.

There's a phrase in Paul's letter to the Romans that seems appropriate. He says that the "whole creation has been groaning in labor pains until now" (Romans 8:22). I doubt if Paul had our modern environmental concerns in mind, but perhaps there's something to be said here about listening to nature's groans for God's voice. If so, how might we listen for this voice?

I'm not a scientist and don't pretend to be one. Instead, I'm a pastor, trained in theology, who is concerned about what some consider to be a war between religion and science, but over the years I have invited my congregations to observe Evolution Weekend, which falls near Charles Darwin's birthday (February 12), as I see it, is a call for people of faith and people of science to listen to each other for the good of the planet.

As a Christian, I look to the Bible for a word from God, and in doing this I'm no different than people of most religious faiths, who also turn to their sacred scriptures to hear that voice of guidance. While looking first to Scripture, I believe God has other ways of speaking to us. Perhaps God is speaking to us in the groans of the world, inviting us to do something redemptive. If so, then how might we interpret these groans? What tools would we need to make sense of them?

I've come to the conclusion that if we're going to hear this voice, we must turn to science. Unfortunately, many people of faith have become jaded about science. Having been led both by some religious teachers and by some scientists to believe they must choose – the Bible or the Science Book – they choose the Bible and neglect science. Indeed, not only do they neglect it, they revile it. So, when scientists tell us that the earth is warming in ways that are destructive, many of us won't listen. As a result of our inability to hear nature's cry, we continue to overuse, misuse, and destroy the earth.

Seeking a sense of balance, I've developed a new appreciation for the message of Genesis 1. It tells us first that the created order is good, and second, that we're to be good stewards of this created order. Older translations speak of dominion, a word that has been taken as permission to despoil the earth, but I believe the intent of the passage is different. It is a call to tend to the needs of creation and live in peace with it.

It's the sense of urgency about the state of nature that led me to embrace this move to bridge the gap between faith and science, and become an early signer of the *Clergy Letter Concerning Religion and Science* (being one of more than 11,000 persons to do so). It's why I have encouraged the congregations I've served to observe Evolution Weekend.

In light of this urgency that I have felt, I ask the question: "Can we hear God's voice speaking to us through nature's voice?" If so, then what is God saying? Perhaps it is this: "Be good stewards of my creation." Then, as we seek to be good stewards, perhaps we could start the process by simply replacing an incandescent bulb or two with a CFL bulb. We could decide to drive a smaller car or carpool. If we all do something, then together we can make a difference in the fate of the created order.

AFTERWORD

Faith is personal. It's rooted in traditions passed on from one generation to another. It is influenced by our ethnic and national backgrounds, but is also influenced by the way we interact with each other. History shows that religion can have both a negative and a positive impact on society. It's often difficult to separate out nationalist and religious ideologies. In the course of these varied essays I have tried to offer a broad and inclusive vision for the way in which religion and faith can exist on the public square. For faith to operate effectively in our context, people of faith must understand that their actions and arguments must never be undertaken in a coercive fashion.

Quite often our faith-influenced values must be restated in what looks like secular clothing. It's not a matter of hiding the foundations of one's views, but recognizing that for these values to have effect in society they must become shared values. If we demand that this or that practice have precedence because it is decreed in the Bible or the Qur'an or any other sacred text, then we will have failed in our efforts. Of course, when we engage in the conversation we can share the origins of our values and why they mean so much to us, but we cannot impose a religion on another person. This has, of course, been tried many times and in many places, but it has been deemed a failure.

May we then bring our traditions into the conversation in the pursuit of justice for all, recognizing that standing at the heart of the American experiment is the belief encapsulated by the motto *E Pluribus Unum* – Out of the Many One.

BIBLIOGRAPHY

Abbott, Lyman. *Reminences,* Boston: Houghton-Mifflin Company, 1915.

Bevere, Allan. *Politics of Witness: The Character of the Church in the World.* (Gonzalez, FL: Energion Publications, 2011.

Cornwall, Robert D. *Ultimate Allegiance: The Subversive Nature of the Lord's Prayer.* Gonzalez, FL: Energion Publications, 2010.

Cornwall, Robert D. and Arthur Gross Schaefer, "Faith and Politics: Finding a Way to Have a Fruitful Conversation." *Congregations* (Summer 2008): 27-30.

Curry, Thomas J. *Farewell to Christendom: The Future of Church and State in America.* New York: Oxford University Press, 2001.

Eck, Diana. *A New Religious America: How a "Christian Country" Has Become the World's Most Religiously Diverse Nation.* San Francisco: Harper One, 2001.

Elnes, Eric. *Asphalt Jesus: Finding a New Christian Faith along the Highways of America.* San Franciso: Jossey Bass, 2007.

Elnes, Eric. *The Phoenix Affirmations: A New Vision for the Future of Christianity.* San Francisco: Jossey Bass, 2007.

Fea, John. *Was America Founded as a Christian Nation? A Historical Introduction.* Louisville: Westminster John Knox Press, 2011.

Feiler, Bruce. *Abraham: A Journey to the Heart of Three Faiths.* New York: Harper Perennial, 2005.

Gopp, Amy, Christian Piatt, and Brandon Gilvin, Editors. *Split Ticket: Independent Faith in a Time of Partisan Politics.* St. Louis: Chalice Press, 2010.

Hall, Douglas John. *The Cross in Our Context: Jesus and the Suffering World.* Minneapolis, Fortress Press, 2003.

Harris, Sam. *Letter to a Christian Nation.* New York: Knopf, 2006.

Hauerwas, Stanley. *After Christendom: How the Church is to Behave If Freedom, Justice, and a Christian Nation Are Bad Ideas.* Nashville: Abingdon Press, 1991.

Holmes, David. *The Faiths of the Founding Fathers:* New York: Oxford University Press, 2006.

Jewett, Robert and John Shelton Lawrence, *Captain America and the Crusade against Evil.* Grand Rapids: Wm. B. Eerdmans, 2003.

Juergensmeyer, Mark. *Terror in the Mind of God: The Global Rise of Religious Violence.* Third Edition. Berkeley: University of California Press, 2003.

Marty, Martin E. *Building Cultures of Trust.* Grand Rapids: Wm. B. Eeerdmans Publishing Co., 2010.

Meacham, Jon. *American Gospel: God, the Founding Fathers, and the Making of a Nation.* New York: Random House, 2006.

Mead, Walter Russell. *God and Gold: Britain, America, and the Making of the Modern World* New York: Knopf, 2007.

Moltmann, Jürgen. *The Source of Life.* Minneapolis: Fortress Press, 1997.

Moses, John. *The Reluctant Revolutionary: Dietrich Bonhoeffer's Collision with Prusso-German History.* New York: Bergahn Books, 2009.

Neuhaus, Richard John. *The Naked Public Square: Religion and Democracy in America.* Grand Rapids: Wm. B. Eerdmans Publishing Company, 1986.

Palmer, Parker J. *Healing the Heart of Democracy: The Courage to Create a Politics Worthy of the Human Spirit.* San Francisco: Jossey Bass, 2011.

Prothero, Stephen. *Religious Literacy: What Every American Needs to Know – and Doesn't.* San Francisco: Harper One, 2007.

Putnam, Robert D. *American Grace: How Religion Divides and Unites Us.* New York: Simon and Schuster, 2010.

Rasmussen, Larry. Editor. *Reinhold Niebuhr: Theologian of Public Life.* London: Collins Liturgical Publications, 1989.

Rowling, J.K. *Harry Potter and the Deathly Hallows.* New York: Scholastic Books, 2007.

Tillich, Paul. *The Essential Tillich: An Anthology of the Writings of Paul Tillich.* Edited with a Preface by F. Forrester Church. Chicago: University of Chicago Press, 1999.

Tillich, Paul. *The Protestant Era.* Chicago: University of Chicago Press, 1957.

Toulouse, Mark. *God in Public: Four Ways American Christianity and Public Life Relate.* Louisville: WJK Press, 2006.

Wink, Walter. *The Powers that Be: Theology for a New Millennium.* New York: Galilee Books, 1999.

Also by Robert D. Cornwall

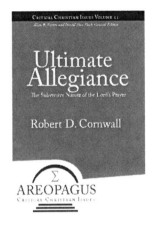

It's a beautiful thing to watch a pastor teaching her or his people with wisdom and grace. In Bob Cornwall's hands the old bones of the Lord's Prayer take breath and life.

— Jason Byassee
Research Fellow in
Theology & Leadership
Duke Divinity School

Also from Energion Publications

Allan Bevere, an ecclesial theologian, combines in this book a wonderful "church as politics" with gospel in a wise, warm, and challenging manner.

— Scot McKnight
Karl A. Olsson Professor
in Religious Studies
North Park University

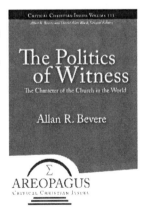

More from Energion Publications

Personal Study

The Jesus Paradigm	David Alan Black	$17.99
Finding My Way in Christianity	Herold Weiss	$16.99
When People Speak for God	Henry Neufeld	$17.99
Holy Smoke, Unholy Fire	Bob McKibben	$14.99
Not Ashamed of the Gospel	Henry Neufeld	$12.99
Evidence for the Bible	Elgin Hushbeck, Jr.	$16.99
Christianity and Secularism	Elgin Hushbeck, Jr.	$16.99
The Messiah and His Kingdom to Come	Bob Makar	$19.99 (B&W)

Christian Living

The Sacred Journey	Chris Surber	$11.99
Directed Paths	Myrtle Neufeld	$7.99
Grief: Finding the Candle of Light	Jody Neufeld	$8.99
Soup Kitchen for the Soul	Renee Crosby	$12.99
Will You Join the Cause of Global Missions?	David Alan Black	$4.99

Bible Study

"In the Original Text It Says"	Ben Baxter	$9.99
Learning and Living Scripture	Geoffrey Lentz	$12.99
The Gospel According to St. Luke: A Participatory Study Guide	Geoffrey Lentz	$8.99
Why Four Gospels?	David Alan Black	$11.99
Philippians: A Participatory Study Guide	Bruce Epperly	$9.99
Ephesians: A Participatory Study Guide	Bob Cornwall	$9.99

Theology

Christian Archy	David Alan Black	$9.99
God's Desire for the Nations	Philip O. Hopkins	$18.99
Ultimate Allegiance	Bob Cornwall	$9.99
History and Christian Faith	Edward W. H. Vick	$9.99
The Adventists' Dilemma	Edward W. H. Vick	$14.99
From Inspiration to Understanding	Edward W. H. Vick	$24.99
Out of This World	Darren McClellan	$24.99
The Questioning God	Ant Greenham	$9.99

Politics

Faith in the Public Square	Bob Cornwall	$16.99
Preserving Democracy	Elgin Hushbeck, Jr.	$14.99

**Energion Publications — P.O. Box 841
Gonzalez, FL 32560**
Website: http://energionpubs.com
Phone: (850) 525-3916

CPSIA information can be obtained at www.ICGtesting.com
Printed in the USA
BVOW071521300712

296559BV00001B/21/P